Volume 3: Implementation Modeling Techniques

Structured Development for Real-Time Systems

D1072933

Volume 3: Implementation Modeling Techniques

Structured Development for Real-Time Systems

by Stephen J. Mellor
& Paul T. Ward

YOURDON PRESS
A Prentice-Hall Company
Englewood Cliffs, New Jersey 07632

Library of Congress Catalog Number 85-50815

Printed in the United States of America

10   9   8   7   6   5   4

ISBN   0-13-854803-X   025

Prentice-Hall International (UK) Limited, *London*
Prentice-Hall of Australia Pty. Limited, *Sydney*
Prentice-Hall Canada Inc., *Toronto*
Prentice-Hall Hispanoamericana, S.A., *Mexico*
Prentice-Hall of India Private Limited, *New Delhi*
Prentice-Hall of Japan, Inc., *Tokyo*
Prentice-Hall of Southeast Asia Pte. Ltd., *Singapore*
Editora Prentice-Hall do Brasil, Ltda., *Rio de Janeiro*

Dedications

To Pamela with Love

   — P.T.W.

To both my families

   — S.J.M.

Acknowledgments

We refer the reader to the acknowledgments for Volume 1 for a list of colleagues to whom we are indebted for contributions to our overall approach.

With respect to Volume 3, we would particularly like to thank Pete Coad, Jr. and Charles S. Hendrickson for their detailed technical reviews. Also, we are grateful to John Shuttleworth, the author of the original version of the SILLY system from which our implementation model derives.

Jean Atelsek served as our primary editor for Volumes 2 and 3, and we are grateful for her perceptive comments and for her patience.

Finally, we thank Gerry Madigan and the Yourdon Press editorial staff.

CONTENTS

Preface

We have divided the model of a system to be developed into two stages, the *essential* model described in Volume 2, and the *implementation* model described in this volume. The division introduces overhead into the modeling process, since the entire content of the essential model must be reorganized and incorporated into the implementation model before addition of details of the implementation technology. Although the overhead of building the model in stages can be reduced by the use of automated support tools for the modeling process, it cannot be eliminated. There is thus a very understandable tendency on the part of systems development teams to eliminate the overhead by building a single-stage system model incorporating both the underlying logic and the implementation details. However, our experience with a large number of development projects indicates that the single-model approach can cause problems, due largely to the necessary involvement of both end-users and automated systems specialists in the development process.

These two groups tend to differ substantially in their perspective on systems development. In the business systems environment, the difference between users and computer specialists is often attributed to the users' lack of technical sophistication. However, this is clearly not the case in the science/engineering arena, where the average end-user (defined as the technical manager, scientist, or engineer responsible for the area within which an embedded system operates) is technically quite sophisticated and probably understands at least the fundamentals of computer technology. The difference in perspective is fundamentally due not to technical sophistication but to different perceptions of the subject matter of embedded systems. The chemical engineer, for example, sees a process control system principally in terms of monitoring and control of reaction variables, optimization of yield, and so on — in other words, in *chemical* terms. The software engineer sees a process control system principally in terms of operation of concurrent tasks, resolution of priority conflicts, and so on — in other words, in *computer* terms. Obviously, the software engineer must be aware of the chemical engineering logic and data structures incorporated into the system. However, the logic and data structures are in a sense "raw materials" to be manipulated by the implementation technology. Similarly, the chemical engineer must be comfortable with aspects of computer technology such as system-user interfaces, but will see them mainly as transportation conduits for chemical data.

The systems modeling process, to be successful, must inherently incorporate *quality assurance* — in other words, both end-users and software engineers must "sign off" on some version of the system model. We are convinced that a single-stage model cannot satisfy the differing needs of end-users and software engineers to understand a proposed system in their own terms. Therefore, the essential-implementation model distinction is a fundamental heuristic, a necessary part of the "style" of applying formal modeling tools to the development process. We urge the systems developers using our approach to try the two model stages, at least on a pilot basis, and to evaluate the results, rather than opting prematurely for a single model.

NOTE ON PRELIMINARY EDITION

We are publishing this preliminary edition in three volumes. The first volume serves as an introduction and describes a set of general tools for modeling the complexities of real-time systems. The second volume addresses the techniques of essential modeling (loosely, systems analysis). It shows how the tools are used to construct a model of what needs to be done. The third volume addresses the techniques of implementation modeling (loosely, systems design). These techniques use the tools described in the introductory volume plus some additional tools to construct a model of the chosen solution.

We are eagerly seeking feedback from our professional colleagues on improvements in presentation and content. We intend to incorporate this feedback into a subsequent edition of this book to be published in the near future.

Section 1
Implementation Modeling Heuristics

The two chapters in this section raise issues that apply to the overall process of creating an implementation model.

Chapter 1, Implementation Modeling Heuristics Overview, introduces a set of guidelines that allow estimation of the quality of an implementation. Chapter 2, Identifying Implementation Constraints, discusses the limits that constrain the application of technology to implement an essential model. An optimum design may be thought of as one that rates as high as possible based on the quality guidelines without violating the implementation constraints.

1
Implementation Modeling Heuristics Overview

1.1 Introduction

It is easy to imagine an environment in which an essential model of a real-time system could be directly implemented. The essential model would be compiled or interpreted into working code exactly like the source code for a high-level language program. In addition to the localized decisions made by a typical compiler, the essential model compiler would make decisions with a broader scope. The compiler, for example, would distribute executable instructions among a set of target machines, organizing the code for each target machine into an optimal set of concurrent tasks.

Alas, a general-purpose real-time implementation environment with this broad a scope has not yet been created. Consequently the systems modeling process must go beyond the essential model and describe details of the implementation. This chapter presents a set of guidelines for implementation modeling, guidelines that are quite different from the essential modeling heuristics presented in Volume 2. The differences stem from a fundamental distinction between essential models and implementation models — the essential model is an *original* creation, while the implementation model is *derived* from the essential model. Because of this distinction, implementation modeling heuristics all take some feature of the essential model as a point of reference.

The guidelines we will present in this chapter are minimization of essential model distortion, satisfactory approximation to essential model behavior, top-down allocation to implementation technology, classification of the essential model by implementation resources, and data abstraction from the essential model. These provide an overall framework for our approach to implementation modeling and underlie many of the more specific guidelines to be presented in the following chapters.

1.2 Minimization of essential model distortion

A *distortion* of an essential model is a change in its organization based on some criterion other than the system's subject matter. Take as an example an essential model that includes the periodic modification of a satellite's attitude based on some pre-arranged schedule. This portion of the model can be thought of as the essential response to New Satellite Attitude is Required, and is represented by Figure 1.1.

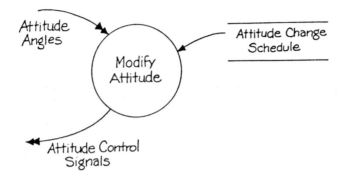

Figure 1.1 Essential model fragment — satellite attitude modification.

In a contemporary satellite, the logic to perform this job would probably be implemented on a single on-board microprocessor. There is in this case no distortion of the essential model; a single essential model element (an event response) translates into a single implementation element (a task within a processor) and thus the essential model organization is preserved. Except for a comment indicating the technology choice, the implementation model would be identical to Figure 1.1.

The implementation of attitude modification would have been quite different in one of the early satellites. Because of the weight and delicacy of early 1960's processor hardware, control of satellites was typically performed via telemetry from a ground station. The model in Figure 1.2 illustrates this more distorted implementation strategy. The single essential model element has become two separate elements of the implementation, the I/O circuitry on the satellite and the control logic on the ground. A partitioning, a new interface, and a synchronization requirement have been introduced, none of which are required by the system's basic subject matter.

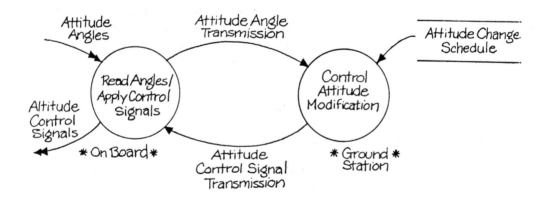

Figure 1.2 Distorted implementation of modification for early satellites.

The heuristic of minimum distortion states that, all other things being equal, an implementation with less distortion of the essential model is better than one with greater distortion. In the two examples cited above, of course, all other things are *not* equal — modern processors allow for less distortion of this essential model than did the processors of the early 1960's. There are two reasons for the usefulness of this criterion. First, the essential model, by definition, is the clearest possible picture of the required behavior of the system. An implementation model with the same structure as the essential model is therefore the clearest possible implementation. In addition, since the success of an implementation model depends on its verifiability, the quality assurance process will be more effective if the implementation model differs as little as possible from the essential model. Second, the essential model is constructed with minimal interfaces. An implementation that respects these interfaces is desirable, since interfaces are typically the most vulnerable part of a system [1].

1.3 Satisfactory approximation to essential model behavior

The essential model contains no implementation details, or, to put it another way, the essential model assumes ideal implementation technology. Consider Figure 1.3, which is extracted from the Defect Inspection System essential model (Appendix D in Volume 2). The figure can be interpreted as, When the edge of the sheet is under the chopper, the Chop signal will be issued at that very instant. The ideal of zero time delay cannot be realized by actual implementation technology — it can only be *approximated*. Therefore any implementation strategy must be evaluated as to its ability to provide a satisfactory approximation to the ideal, by calculation, simulation, or experimentation. In Figure 1.3, for example, suppose that the operation of the chopper requires the activation of a task. In a multitasking implementation, the activation of a higher-priority task could delay chopper operation and thus affect product quality.

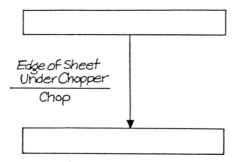

Figure 1.3 Essential model idealization.

The assumption of zero response time is only one of the idealizations of the essential model. The control and data flows on the model are assumed to travel at infinite speed, and the stores on the essential model are assumed to have unlimited memory capacity.

The heuristic of satisfactory approximation to essential model behavior states that each idealization made within the essential model must be identified, and the approximation achieved by the corresponding portion of the proposed implementation must be evaluated. In some cases the evaluation is straightforward. The permissible delay-time limits corresponding to Figure 1.3 are a function of the chopper characteristics, the conveyer speed, and the required sheet size tolerance. In other cases, however, it is not easy to determine when an approximation is satisfactory. Some approximations involve not satisfaction of requirements but ease of use or economy of operation. Human-computer interfaces, for instance, are notoriously "soft" in terms of response-time limit determination.

1.4 Top-down allocation to implementation technology

We will use the term *allocation* to refer to a mapping of some portion of an essential model to a unit of implementation technology. Figures 1.1 and 1.2 in this chapter illustrate an allocation; the event response of Figure 1.1 is mapped into the on-board I/O circuitry and into a task in a ground-based computer.

The heuristic of top-down allocation in its simplest form merely states that allocation to higher-level implementation units should precede allocation to lower-level ones. In practice, however, applying this criterion requires techniques for carrying out the allocation (which will be discussed in Chapters 3 and 4) and a classification scheme for implementation units. We have classified implementation units into three stages or levels — the processor stage, the task stage, and the module stage.* The overall organization of the implementation model is based on these stages.

A *processor* is a person or a machine that can carry out instructions and store data. (The human as a potential processor is not a typical focus of real-time systems development. Nevertheless, using a human processor is sometimes the most feasible way of implementing a portion of an essential model). Machines that may be processors run the gamut from simple analogue or digital circuits through microprocessors to minis, mainframes, and "supercomputers." The processor stage of the implementation model is represented as a network of processors to which the essential model has been allocated. Because a processor provides its own execution and storage resources, true concurrency of operation is possible within this stage; all the processors may be active simultaneously.

A *task* is a set of instructions that is manipulated (started, stopped, interrupted, and resumed) as a unit by the system software of a processor. Batch programs, on-line interactive tasks, and interrupt handlers all qualify as tasks under our definition. The task stage of the implementation model is represented as a set of networks of tasks, one

---

*In the first printing of Volume 1, Chapter 5, The Modeling Process, we referred to these three stages as the Processor Environment Model, the Process Environment Model, and the Procedure Organization Model, respectively.

network per processor. Each task network describes the distribution to individual tasks of the portion of the essential model carried out by a processor. A task depends on the processor within which it operates for execution and storage resources. Therefore a task network can be capable of concurrency of operation if the processor has multiple CPUs, or if the processor shares its resources among the tasks to simulate concurrency.

A *module* is a set of instructions that is activated as a unit by the control logic within a task in a mutually exclusive fashion (only one module may be active at a time); subprograms, functions, subroutines, and procedures all qualify as modules under our definition. This definition of a module obviously precludes concurrency among the modules within a task. The module stage of the implementation model is represented as a set of module hierarchies, one hierarchy per task. Each module hierarchy describes the distribution to individual modules of the portion of the essential model carried out by the task.

Figure 1.4 suggests the overall structure of an implementation model. Notice that the processor stage and the task stage may each correspond to multiple levels within a leveled set of transformation schemas (Volume 1, Chapters 6 and 12). As an example, a transformation within the task stage may represent either an individual task, or a group of tasks with some common characteristics.

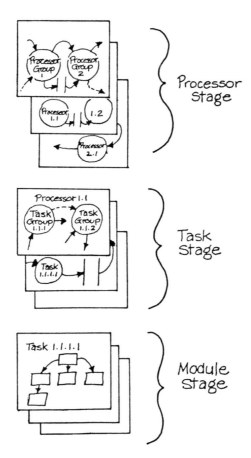

Figure 1.4 Implementation model structure.

The classification scheme just described clearly doesn't fit all implementation environments perfectly; it is itself implementation-dependent. An analog circuit, for example, has no internal structure corresponding clearly to a task or module stage. An element of computation within an array processor, to take another example, may be neither a task nor a module, but is an important unit of organization. It is possible that future developments in implementation technology will render part or all of this scheme obsolete. Nevertheless, we feel that the framework presented here will be useful for the majority of real-time implementations for the near future.

Top-down allocation is a useful heuristic because the great complexity of constructing a typical implementation model requires mapping the essential model onto an implementation in stages. One of the most complex tasks is allocating so as to ensure that portions of the model requiring concurrent execution are not assigned to elements of the technology prohibiting concurrency. The stages we have described are based on concurrency characteristics, with the processor stage being truly concurrent, the task stage simulating concurrency, and the module stage prohibiting concurrency. In this way, one of the most difficult problems of real-time system design — namely, the correct management of concurrency — can be approached by progressively modifying the concurrency shown on the essential model to account for the concurrency characteristics of the implementation technology.

1.5 Classification of the essential model by use of implementation resources

The previous section alluded to techniques for the allocation process, but did not describe the rationale for a particular allocation decision. On what basis, for example, does a developer decide to use two microprocessors rather than one for a particular implementation? We describe the decision-making process as *classification by use of implementation resources*. The type of classification referred to is an organization of portions of the essential model by a criterion related to implementation technology rather than to the system's subject matter. The classification can be based on either qualitative or quantitative grounds.

As an example of qualitative classification, consider the overall configuration of a remote data entry terminal. An implementer might choose two microprocessors with very different characteristics, one with an extended arithmetic instruction set to handle local computations, and a "stripped-down" micro to handle data communications. This choice implies a classification of the associated essential model into those portions that involve arithmetic and those that do not — a classification that may have little relationship to the essential model's organization but that will influence allocation decisions.

Quantitative classification can be illustrated by the need to distribute a process control system among two microprocessors in order to avoid processor overload. Here the microprocessors have the same qualitative characteristics, but neither has the processing power to run the entire system. This distribution requirement implies a classification of essential model transformations according to their "weight" in contributing to processor load. As with the case of the arithmetic and non-arithmetic micros, this classification is relevant for allocation but unrelated to the essential model's organization.

In addition to the distinction between qualitative and quantitative classification, there are characteristically different classifications at different stages of the implementation model. Classification at the processor stage will typically involve physical characteristics of the hardware — available instruction set, proximity to the physical environment of the system, and so on. Task-level classification may be made on the basis of activation and timing aspects of a task. Classification at the module level is more likely to focus on logical or mathematical characteristics, such as common use of a parsing or integration algorithm or a table structure.

The heuristic of classification by use of implementation resources states that at each stage of the model it is necessary to identify the relevant implementation resources, and to use the resulting classification to guide the allocation process. The criterion is useful because it allows the designer to maximize the use of expensive resources.

1.6 Data abstraction from the essential model

The essential model is organized around a natural level of detail for a system, that of responses to external events and of groupings of closely related responses. It is possible, by examining an essential model, to identify alternate possibilities for organization. Some of these alternate organizations can be quite subject-matter specific. Consider two events from the Bottle-Filling System essential model (Appendix B in Volume 2), Operator Turns Line On and Operator Removes Bottle. The portion of the response to these two events that involves checking the weight sensor and the bottle contact is identical. By identifying portions of the two event responses as a single unit, we have generalized to create a *data abstraction* [2], consisting of the weight and bottle contact readings, around which we may organize a portion of the implementation.

Consider another data abstraction, this one involving the SILLY system (Appendix C in Volume 2). Displaying the trigger word and displaying a logic state are closely related, since the logic state composition (0 or 1 for each channel) is a subset of the trigger word composition (0, 1, or "don't care" for each channel). The data composite consisting of the trigger word and the logic state could be displayed by common processing logic. The abstraction here is somewhat broader in scope than the previous one, since it treats as a unit two data elements that were considered separate in the essential model.

An abstraction may be broad enough in scope so as not to be subject-matter specific. Consider a "display line" derived from the SILLY system, but defined as any set of characters that could be displayed on one line of a display. An abstraction this broad could define processing logic that is completely application-independent.

The heuristic of data abstraction from the essential model states that the essential model should be searched for common elements that will identify potential implementation resources. Note that this criterion starts from the essential model rather than from an existing resource but ultimately has the same goal as classification of implementation resources — that is, effective resource utilization.

1.7 Conflicts among heuristics

A close examination of the heuristics just presented reveals many possibilities for conflict. For example, allocating the portions of the essential model involving complex arithmetic to a separate processor may optimize the use of processor resources but distort the organization of the essential model considerably. Implementation modeling is critically important for visualizing and exploring the consequences of such conflicts. In fact, one can define implementation modeling as the process of finding an optimum resolution among a set of conflicting objectives. Formulating this optimization problem analytically is beyond our abilities — this is the fundamental reason why an "essential model compiler" is not currently available. However, the modeling tools presented in Volume 1 and the heuristics presented in this volume make the problem solvable by systems developers.

1.8 Summary

The creation of an implementation model is fundamentally an activity of derivation, of mapping the contents of an essential model into an implementation environment. This mapping process is most effective when guided by implementation modeling heuristics. In this chapter, we have set out the heuristics that we feel are most broadly applicable. In the remaining chapters of this volume we will explore the application of these guidelines in more detail to specific modeling situations.

Chapter 1: References

1.   G. M. Weinberg, *An Introduction to General Systems Thinking.* New York: John Wiley & Sons, 1975.

2.   M.L. Brodie and S.N. Zilles (eds). Proceedings: Workshop on Data Abstraction, Databases and Conceptual Modeling. SIGPLAN Notices 16, 1 (1981).

Identifying Implementation Constraints

2.1 Introduction

One of the most consistent complaints about graphics-based modeling techniques has been that they are "incomplete" in terms of specification of quantitative details. A rigorous model of a system to be developed clearly must be complete in a quantitative sense as well as in a qualitative sense. However, the specification of quantitative details is often hampered by a confusion about implementation-dependence. For example, if three input signals must be sampled at the same rate and processed over the same time interval, the equation in Figure 2.1 expresses a constraint that applies *only* if the signal processing is sequenced within a single task. Consider the situation where a processor is allocated to each signal, or where a single processor can effectively overlap the signal processing tasks (for example, if they are I/O bound). The constraints are then

$$T_{P1} \leq T_1 - T_o,$$
$$T_{P2} \leq T_1 - T_o,$$
$$T_{P3} \leq T_1 - T_o$$

— a much less demanding situation.

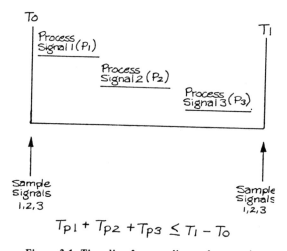

$$T_{P1} + T_{P2} + T_{P3} \leq T_1 - T_o$$

Figure 2.1 Time line for sampling and processing.

The separation of essential and implementation models can resolve much of the confusion about the specification of quantitative constraints. We will define an *implementation constraint* as a bound placed on some measurement of system performance that results from a choice of implementation technology. This implies that the determination of implementation constraints must go hand-in-hand with implementation modeling. It also implies that some quantitative constraints do not depend on implementation technology and thus should be associated with the essential model. We shall refer to these as *environmental constraints*.

In the following sections, we will explore the identification of various implementation constraints based on the structure of the essential model and on other data about the system's environment.

2.2 Implementation constraints versus resource availability

Physical implementation resources such as primary and secondary memory size, instruction speed, communication rate, and so on are typically available in fixed-size increments, providing a resource availability profile that is a step function, as in the example of Figure 2.2. For a resource of this type, it is necessary to identify the maximum resource size obtainable. In the case of primary memory, this maximum resource size might be the largest memory made, the largest memory purchasable within the project budget, or the largest memory meeting size and weight restrictions.

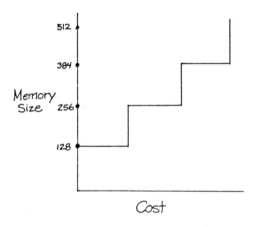

Figure 2.2 Primary memory size versus cost.

The approach to implementation constraints will differ according to the relationship between the order of magnitude of resource usage $O(u)$ and the order of magnitude of maximum obtainable resource size $O(s)$. If $O(u) > O(s)$, the implementation is not feasible and alternate strategies must be explored. In the case of processor instruction speed, for example, an order-of-magnitude overload will force consideration of multiprocessor configurations. If $O(u) < O(s)$, there is a potential resource excess, and precise implementation constraints related to the availability of the resource need not be calculated. If the average of executed instructions per task for an eight-user system is 50,000, context-switching is very efficient, and secondary memory access time is negligible, a 4-MIPS processor can complete a user task in about 10^{-2} seconds. This is so fast by human response standards that specifying required response times is irrelevant. A slower processor may well be adequate, but the decision should be deferred if possible until actual performance measurements are available. Only if $O(u) = O(s)$ is a careful consideration of implementation constraints justified.

2.3 Environmental information required to determine constraints

Implementation constraints must often be derived from information about the system's environment. The context schema (Volume 2, Chapter 2) provides a useful base from which to prepare an inventory of such information.

The input and output flows on a context schema have measurable characteristics that implementation strategies must account for. It is convenient to examine the characteristics of discrete flows separately from those of continuous flows. The relevant characteristics for discrete flows are:

- flow size (number of bits per flow)

- average rate of occurrence

- maximum rate of occurrence (burst rate)

- required retention time (if the system must store the flow internally as an identifiable unit).

For continuous flows, the important characteristics are:

- range (or maximum amplitude)

- signal-to-noise ratio

- frequency profile (identification of the highest-frequency meaningful component of variation).

Although these parameters are not required to create a verifiable essential model, they are independent of implementation technology and thus can conveniently be attached to the essential model's data specification.

2.4 Essential model transformations as sources of implementation constraints

The portion of the essential model dealing with transformations (transformation schemas, data transformation specifications, and control transformation specifications), if carefully constructed, can serve as a framework for identification of implementation constraints dealing with timing. Consider Figure 2.3, which is a fragment extracted from the Bottle-Filling System (Appendix B in Volume 2). Let's first examine an element of timing that is implementation-independent. The real-world Filling Bottle state is delimited by the opening and closing of the bottle-filling valve, at rates chosen to minimize filling time while permitting sufficient precision in the amount placed in the bottle. The duration of the Filling Bottle state is driven by the physical characteristics of the bottle-filling machinery. No change in the implementation technology of the embedded system can cause the bottle to fill faster while maintaining precision, and the idea of an implementation constraint does not apply.

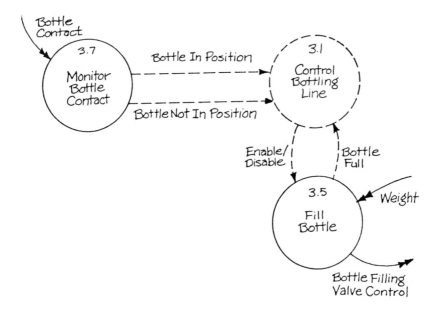

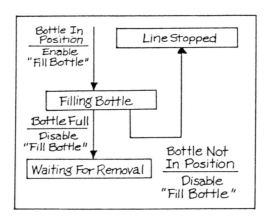

Figure 2.3 Portion of bottling system essential model.

Let's now examine the transition between Filling Bottle and Line Stopped, labeled with the condition Bottle Not In Position and the action Disable "Fill Bottle" (the "disabling" is assumed to mean the initiation of closing of the valve at its maximum rate). The transition would be triggered by a premature removal of the bottle during filling, for instance, by the operator knocking the bottle over. According to the essential model, the transition takes zero time. In practice, the time duration is completely dependent on the implementation technology of the embedded system. Consider the following set of possible implementations:

1. A processor is dedicated to monitoring the bottle contact and initiating valve closure as necessary.

2. The Bottle Out Of Position condition causes a highest-priority interrupt in a processor dedicated to a single bottling line, and activates a task that initiates valve closure.

3. A Monitor Bottle Contact task runs on a time-available basis in a processor serving several lines. A Bottle Out Of Position condition causes the task to set a flag, which initiates valve closing the next time the Fill Bottle task is activated.

In implementation 1, the actual transition time would be only a few microseconds at typical processor instruction speeds. In implementation 3, the servicing of a number of tasks might intervene between the time the condition occurs and when the action is taken. If the amount of spillage is of concern to the system builders (say if the liquid is toxic), a constraint on the maximum permissible transition time is appropriate and will have direct impact on the choice of implementation.

We will generalize the preceding discussion by listing the elements of the transformation model whose duration is implementation-independent and those whose duration is implementation-dependent. Implementation-independent elements include:

• durations of states other than unlabeled "transitory" states, and

• durations of data transformations that are enabled and disabled.

Implementation-dependent elements (i.e., elements that may be subject to implementation constraints) include:

• durations of unlabeled "transitory" states,

• durations of transitions between states,

• intervals between discrete inputs and discrete outputs of data transformations,

• intervals between triggering and discrete outputs of data transformations, and

• intervals between a change in value of a continuous input and the corresponding output of a data transformation.

Note that the last item is one determinant of the required sampling rate for a digital implementation, which is discussed in more detail in Chapter 4, Task Modeling.

2.5 Essential model data as a source of implementation constraints

The portion of the essential model dealing with stored data (the data schema, the stores on the transformation schema, and the data specifications) can also motivate implementation constraints. These constraints will be requirements for availability of primary memory, secondary memory, or both. Required data storage volumes can be derived from the environmental data discussed in Section 2.3 of this chapter. To determine the storage volume corresponding to an object type on an entity-relationship diagram, it is necessary to know:

- the size of the input flows from which instances of the object type are created,

- the rate of arrival of these input flows,

- the required retention time of these input flows, and

- the rate of arrival of any flow that deletes instances of the object type.

Consider as an example a portion of an air-traffic control system that stores data about each aircraft currently within an airspace. Assume that aircraft enter the airspace at a maximum rate of ten per minute, stay in the airspace for a maximum of one hour, and require 1 kilobyte of stored data each. In the worst case, 600 aircraft can enter the airspace before the first one leaves, requiring 600 kilobytes of memory.

Relationships on an entity-relationship diagram also generate data storage volume, since a relationship must be implemented as a pointer or as embedded data. This volume can be significant if data storage categories are heavily interconnected, and so the same questions must be asked for the relationship as for the object type.

2.6 Summary

Quantitative constraints on the performance of implementation technology are critical to a successful implementation. The separation of the essential and implementation models can be used to advantage to identify the constraints that are required by a specific implementation strategy.

Section 2

Processor and Task Stage Heuristics

The five chapters of this section examine the implementation modeling process as it applies to the selection of a hardware configuration and to the selection of software organization within a hardware unit. The section divides naturally into two subsections, the first, consisting of Chapters 3, 4, and 5, dealing with application-specific issues and the second, consisting of Chapters 6 and 7, dealing with system support issues.

Chapter 3, Processor Modeling, considers the problems involved in hardware configuration selection and the guidelines that can resolve those problems.

Chapter 4, Task Modeling, examines the complexities of multitasking implementations and suggests approaches to managing those complexities.

Chapter 5, Interface Modeling, discusses the modeling implications of processor and task allocation with respect to defining the interfaces created by the allocation process.

Chapter 6, Modeling System Services — Process Management, establishes guidelines for selecting an optimum set of system utilities to support the processing done by the system to be built.

Chapter 7, Modeling System Services — Data Management, introduces a similar set of guidelines, in this case directed to supporting a proposed system's data access needs.

3
Processor Modeling

3.1 Introduction

The first stage in translating the essential model into a picture of the desired implementation is to identify the processors that will carry out the work of the system. It is then possible to reorganize the essential model around the processors chosen. The resulting model has the same content as the essential model, and predicts the same system behavior, but has a different upper-level partitioning. Figure 3.1 suggests the difference in organization between the two models. Note that the transformation schema notation is used differently in the two models; in the essential model a transformation may only represent a portion of the work done by the system, while in the processor stage of the implementation model a transformation may *also* represent a person or machine that carries out part of the work.

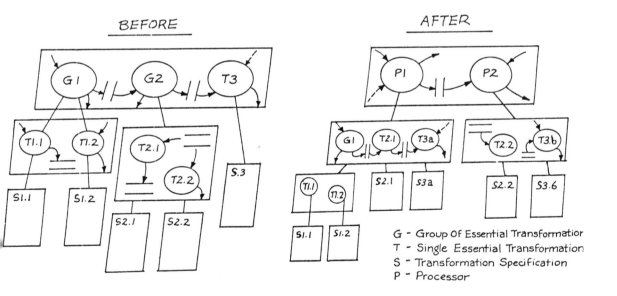

Figure 3.1 The reorganization process.

The reorganization can affect the essential model at any level; referring again to Figure 3.1, the transformation T3 has been partitioned into two pieces, and the corresponding specification has been split between two upper-level portions of the processor stage.

In the following sections, we will first examine the criteria for reorganization and then examine the details of the reorganization process.

3.2 Allocation criteria

Reorganization into the processor model results from a comparison of features of a candidate processor to features of the essential model. The simplest case of reorganization involves allocating the entire essential model to a single processor. The criterion in this case is that the candidate processor be capable of carrying out all the work described by the essential model. If there is more than one candidate processor adequate to the job, a selection based on secondary factors (cost, ease of upgrading, and so on) must be made.

In the more general case, the contents of the essential model are to be allocated among a set of candidate processors. The choice of processors may be based on qualitative distinctions, such as the availability in a particular processor of an extended arithmetic instruction set, array processing capability, or the ability to interface to a particular type of peripheral device. The choice may also be based on quantitative distinctions, such as speed, primary memory capacity, or secondary memory capacity. Finally, the choice may be based on some characteristic of the system's environment. In the case of a surveillance satellite system, for example, the perception/action space might contain elements (surveillance analysts, on-board camera equipment) that are widely separated geographically. Communications bandwidth or communications cost, and size/weight criteria may thus dictate a distribution of function between on-board and ground-based computers.

Let's examine a portion of the essential model for the SILLY system (Appendix C of Volume 2) from the point of view of required speed. The transformations Control Acquisition, Check for Trigger Word, and Record Logic State must be able to operate at the frequency of the Clock Pulse event flow. If the clock pulse occurs at the rate of 1 megahertz, a 1- or 2-MIPS microprocessor could not complete an acquisition cycle rapidly enough to keep pace.

The preceding analysis suggests that a very fast processor is required to do the work described by the essential model. However, the transformations Record Trigger Word and Display Trigger Word need not operate at this fast pace; the speed required is only that of normal keyboard/display processing. Furthermore, the work done by the faster transformations is simple in nature and does not require the capabilities of a general-purpose processor. A reasonable choice might be a pair of processors, a slower general-purpose microprocessor to handle keyboard/display interactions, and a high-speed, special-purpose digital circuit for logic acquisition.

In a multiprocessor allocation, it is possible for the allocation criteria determined by processor characteristics to conflict with the essential model structure. The example of Figure 3.2 does not suffer from this problem; the transformations can cleanly be assigned to either the fast processor or the slow processor. However, this is not true in general.

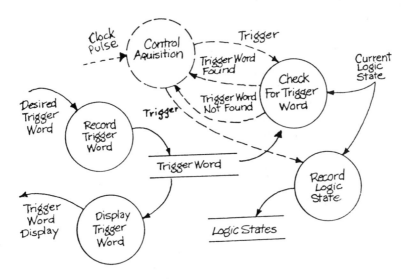

Figure 3.2 Portion of SILLY essential model.

The most serious form of conflict is caused by the need to split a data transformation representing a single event response among two or more processors. Take as an example Figure 3.3, which is extracted from the Bottle-Filling System essential model (Appendix B in Volume 2). When Control Area is enabled, monitoring of pH is active and changing the setpoint is prohibited. When the area is disabled, the reverse is true.

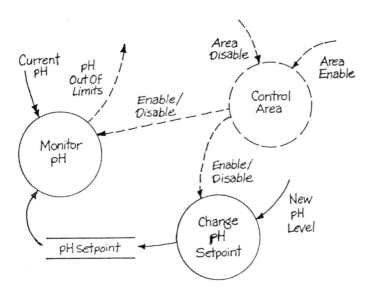

Figure 3.3 Portion of bottle-filling system essential model.

Consider two possible allocations of the Change pH Setpoint transformation: In the first, the pH Setpoint data is shared between two processors, and the acceptance and storage of a New pH Level takes place within a single processor; in the second, the acceptance of the New pH Level takes place in one processor, but the memory and thus the storage activity is localized to a second processor.

The two allocations are illustrated in Figures 3.4 and 3.5. In both cases, there is a synchronization requirement between Change pH Setpoint and the handling of the Area Enable event flow; if the Control Area is disabled and a New pH Level is entered, the data must be placed in storage before an Area Enable is honored. However, in Figure 3.4 the synchronization is entirely confined to Processor 2, provided that Processor 1 isn't using the shared memory during the period when the area is disabled. In Figure 3.5, the synchronization requires the resources of both processors; once a New pH Level is submitted, the Accepted New pH Level must be both sent and stored before an Area Enable can be honored.

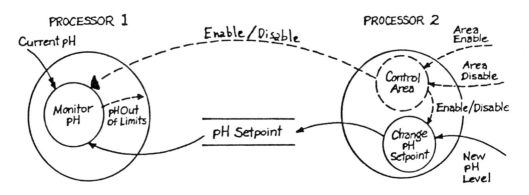

Figure 3.4 Allocation of change pH setpoint to one processor.

In addition to the increased synchronization requirement, the allocation shown in Figure 3.5 disperses the logic of an event response between code in two processors. A change to the event response is more difficult to implement in this situation than if the logic were localized to a single processor.

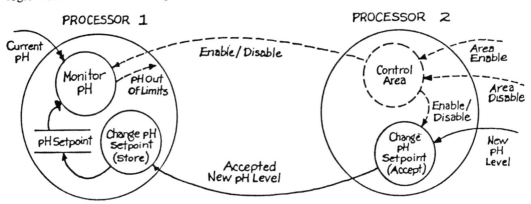

Figure 3.5 Allocation of change pH setpoint to one processor.

We are *not* suggesting that allocations like that of Figure 3.5 are always to be avoided. We *are* suggesting, however, that the costs and benefits of effective use of processor resources versus essential model distortion be taken into account carefully before such decisions are made.

In a complex situation, it is unlikely that the first allocation scheme chosen is likely to be the final one. Allocation should be regarded as an iterative process that allows the visualization and evaluation of alternatives.

3.3 Identification of processors

As we mentioned in the introduction, processors are represented as high-level transformations on a transformation schema. The name given to a processor should highlight the *role* played by the processor in the computation rather than its manufacturer, model number, or other physical characteristics. "Temperature Control Micro" is a much more helpful name than "Zip Zap 8000-2Meg" for the purposes of the processor stage of the implementation model.

Another aspect of identification is the distinction between a *single piece of hardware* and a single *processor*. As we will use the term in this discussion, we willl identify a single processor from the point of view of the writer of the application code. Consider a configuration consisting of a set of CPUs managed by a multitasking operating system. The operating system activates tasks as required to a "server" (CPU) based on load-leveling considerations. This configuration would be a single processor from the point of view of the implementation model; a coder would be writing code not for a specific CPU but for the entire configuration.

The distinction between a piece of hardware and a processor also applies to the provision of redundant and backup processors for an implementation. The combination of an "active" and a "warm-standby" computer would be represented as a single processor.

Sometimes a decision is made to embed some of a system's logic within a sensor or actor. This means that the sensor or actor must appear as a processor within the implementation, and can lead to a situation like the one in Figure 3.6. This figure represents a variation on the Bottle-Filling System (Appendix B in Volume 2) in which the pH is provided as a set of values from an array of sensors and must be averaged to obtain current pH. The pH sensor device appears in the overall model twice, as a terminator (source of data) on the essential model context schema and as a processor (manipulator of data) on the implementation model. In Figure 3.6 the essential activity of monitoring the average pH by checking individual sensor values is split between the averaging logic and the pH Control Micro.

People who provide input data to systems often serve as both terminators and as processors by carrying out manual data entry procedures. The inclusion of such manual processors within the processor level provides a convenient vehicle for integrating data entry procedures into the overall system model.

A final consideration on processor identification concerns processors that simply move data from place to place within a multiprocessor configuration. Examples of such processors are message switchers, keyboard handlers, and display handlers. Such processors are often "visible" to the application code only in terms of a low-level call protocol. If this is true, the processor in question should be omitted from the model, since no essential model activities or data are allocated to it.

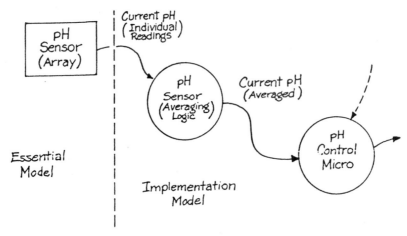

Figure 3.6 A sensor acting as both terminator and processor.

3.4 Allocation of the transformation model

Now that we have discussed the decision-making processes that lead to allocation, let's examine the details of the allocation process itself. We'll first consider the allocation of the transformations from the essential model and their associated specifics.

The allocation of an entire essential model transformation to a processor means that:

- Data corresponding to the transformation's input flows must be captured by the processor and provided to the code that carries out the transformation;

- Data corresponding to the transformation's output flows must be obtained by the processor from the code that carries out the transformation and sent to the appropriate destination;

- The work described by the transformation must be carried out by code within the processor; and

- Data corresponding to connections between the transformation and a store must be retrieved or placed in storage by the processor.

The allocation process becomes more complex when a low-level transformation (one described by a specification rather than by a lower-level schema) must be split between two or more processors. Let's first consider splitting a data transformation. Figure 3.7 shows a transformation from the Defect Inspection System (Appendix D in Volume 2); its associated specification is:

1.1 Change Current Product

Precondition 1

>   PRODUCT CHANGE occurs

and   STATUS of referenced INSPECTION SURFACE is "off"

Postcondition 1

>   the PRODUCTION RUN referencing the INSPECTION SURFACE indicated
>   by PRODUCT CHANGE contains a reference to the PRODUCT STANDARD
>   in PRODUCT CHANGE

Precondition 2

>   PRODUCT CHANGE occurs

and   STATUS of referenced INSPECTION SURFACE is "on"

Postcondition 2

>   UNABLE TO CHANGE PRODUCT MESSAGE is produced

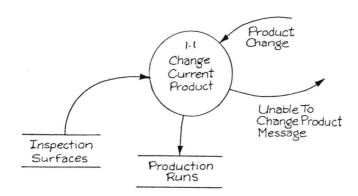

Figure 3.7 A data transformation.

Suppose that this transformation were to be allocated between two processors, an Inspection Surface Micro in possession of the Inspection Surfaces data, and an Operator Console Micro in charge of updating Production Runs and producing the output flow. We will rename the two portions of the original transformation so that we can differentiate the portion of the transformation work that each performs.

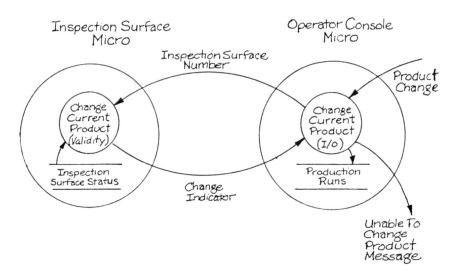

Figure 3.8 Allocation of Figure 3.7.

The results of the allocation are shown in Figure 3.8. The specification for Change Current Product (I/O) is:

Precondition 1

      PRODUCT CHANGE occurs

and   INSPECTION SURFACE NUMBER issued

and   CHANGE INDICATOR is "ok"

Postcondition 1

      The PRODUCTION RUN referencing the INSPECTION SURFACE
      contains a reference to the PRODUCT STANDARD in
      PRODUCT CHANGE

Precondition 2

      PRODUCT CHANGE occurs

and   INSPECTION SURFACE NUMBER issued

and   CHANGE INDICATOR is "not ok"

Postcondition 2

      UNABLE TO CHANGE PRODUCT MESSAGE is produced

The specification for Change Current Product (validity) is:

Precondition 1

INSPECTION SURFACE NUMBER occurs

and   STATUS of referenced INSPECTION SURFACE is "off"

Postcondition 1

CHANGE INDICATOR is "ok"

Precondition 2

INSPECTION SURFACE NUMBER occurs

and   STATUS of referenced INSPECTION SURFACE is "on"

Postcondition 2

CHANGE INDICATOR is "not ok"

In general, to split a transformation specification it is necessary to represent the work done by one part of the specification to the other part. The representation may be in terms of data already manipulated by the other part of the specification, or in terms of flags representing the outcome of logic performed by the other part of the specification.

Now that we've considered splitting a data transformation, let's move on to the splitting of a control transformation. Since the specification for a control transformation (the state transition diagram) has a more regular form than the specification for a data transformation, the splitting procedure can be formalized:

Step 1. Duplicate the state transition diagram for each processor to which part of the control transformation is to be allocated.

Step 2. Check the condition and action(s) for each transition in the state transition diagram copy for each processor, and select the appropriate case:

    2.1   Condition sensed and action taken by this processor: Add an action to signal that the condition has been sensed.

    2.2   Condition sensed by this processor, action taken by another processor: Replace the action by a signal that the condition has been sensed.

    2.3   Condition sensed by another processor, action taken by this processor: Replace the condition by the receipt of a signal that the condition has occurred.

2.4   Condition sensed and action taken by another processor: Replace the condition by the receipt of a signal that the condition has occurred, remove the action.

Step 3. Check each state on each state transition diagram copy.

For each state which fulfills the following conditions:

3.1   All outgoing transitions have conditions that are signals from other processors and no actions.

3.2   All outgoing transitions are directed to a single destination state, whose outgoing transitions in turn all have conditions that are signals from another processor.

Take the following actions:

3.3   Remove the state and its outgoing transitions.

3.4   Reroute the incoming transitions to the destination state.

Apply the procedure iteratively until all possible states have been removed.

Step 4. Remove any actions which are signals with no recipient.

Step 5. Rename states as necessary for clarification.

Let's apply this procedure to the Control Bottling Line transformation from the Bottle-Filling System (Appendix B in Volume 2). The transformation is shown in Figure 3.9 and its associated state transition diagram in Figure 3.10. The transformation will be split between two processors. One (the Fill Control Micro) controls the opening and closing of the Bottle Filling valve and uses the Weight input to determine when the bottle is full. The other (the Mechanical Control Micro) performs the remaining processing (and also has access to the Weight input). Figures 3.11 and 3.12 show the two state transition diagram copies after Step 2 has been applied.

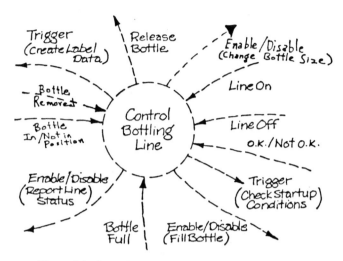

Figure 3.9 Control transformation from bottling system.

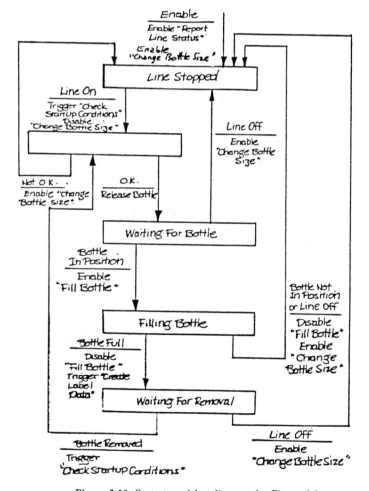

Figure 3.10 State transition diagram for Figure 3.9.

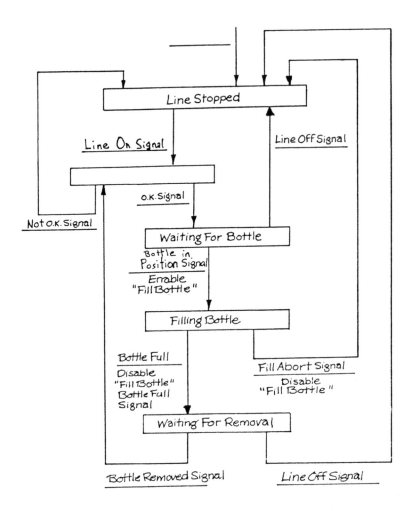

Figure 3.11 Fill control micro state transition diagram after step 2.

Applying Step 3 to Figure 3.11 results in the removal of the Line Stopped state, the unnamed state, and the Waiting for Removal state. Notice that, if Waiting for Removal is examined first, it cannot be removed because it has two destination states. However, it will be removed on the second iteration since the destination states will have been resolved into a single one.

Figures 3.13 and 3.14 show the two state transition diagrams after application of steps 4 and 5. Notice that the ultimate state diagrams satisfy intuitive notions about "which processor needs to know about which state."

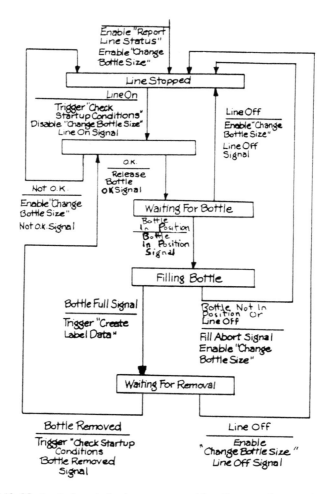

Figure 3.12 Mechanical control micro state transition diagram after step 2.

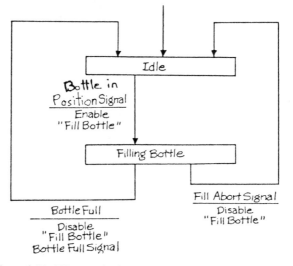

Figure 3.13 Fill control micro state transition diagram — final.

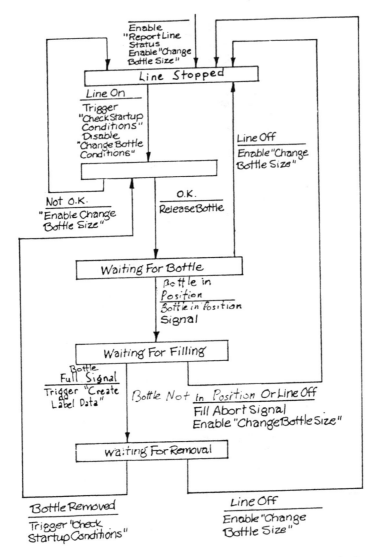

Figure 3.14 Mechanical control micro state transition diagram — final.

3.5 Allocation of the stored data model

Since the stores on the transformation schema correspond to object types and re-lationships on the entity-relationship diagram, allocating the transformation schema provides information that is important for the allocation of stored data. For example, if all transformations that use a store are allocated to a single processor, that processor should normally "own" the store.* However, questions of allocation of stored data must be looked at for each individual object type and relationship to assure complete-ness of the allocation. We therefore recommend using the entity-relationship diagram

---

* An important exception is the provision of a "database backend" processor within a processor configuration, whose job is to store data and manage access for the other processors.

from the essential model to create an entity-relationship diagram for each candidate processor. There are a number of possible mechanisms for making a collection of stored data available to two (or more) processors; we will consider sharing, exclusive ownership, and duplication, using the abstract representation of Figure 3.15.

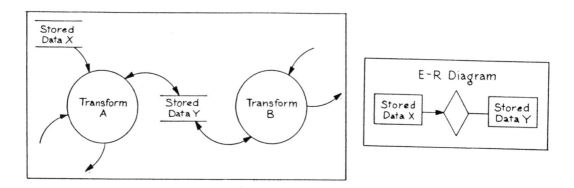

Figure 3.15 Portion of essential model to be allocated.

In the case of *sharing*, a physical data storage mechanism (such as a multiport memory) is accessible to both processors. Although some synchronization is necessary (to prevent both processors from trying to change the same item at the same time) the processors are inherently equal in their ownership of the data. A distributed database manager or a database backend processor, both of which make ownership of the data invisible to the application, would also be modeled as sharing. Figure 3.16 shows sharing of stored data between two processors from the point of view of the leveled transformation schema for the implementation model, and from the point of view of the entity-relationship diagrams for the two processors.

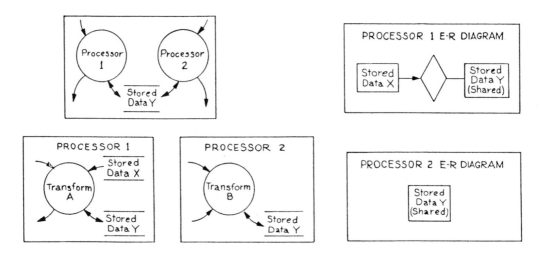

Figure 3.16 Sharing of stored data between twp processors.

In the case of *exclusive ownership,* only one processor has access to the physical data storage mechanism. Therefore the other processor can obtain or modify data only by the cooperation of two processes, one in each processor, that transfer and receive the data. This means that if a transformation does its work in one processor but needs data owned by another processor, *the piece of the transformation that actually accesses storage must be allocated to the other processor.* The modeling of this situation is shown in Figure 3.17. Note that no details of the data transfer mechanism are shown; the topic will be taken up in Chapter 5, Interface Modeling.

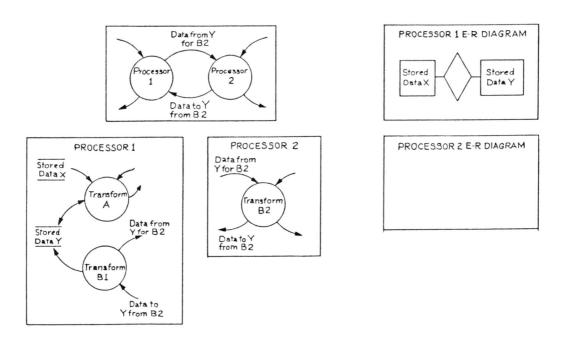

Figure 3.17 Exclusive ownership of stored data by one processor.

Finally, in the case of *duplication,* each processor has access to a data storage mechanism containing a *copy* of the data. Each processor can therefore obtain stored data without the cooperation of the other processor. However, a processor can only *change* stored data with the cooperation of the other processor, since consistency of the duplicate copies must be maintained. If a transformation does its work in one processor but changes data duplicated between its processor and another, a piece of the transformation must be allocated to the other processor to maintain correspondence. The modeling of this situation is shown in Figure 3.18. If the duplication is not exact (some data elements are stored in only one processor) the names of the stores/object types and their associated specifics should be modified to reflect the distinction.

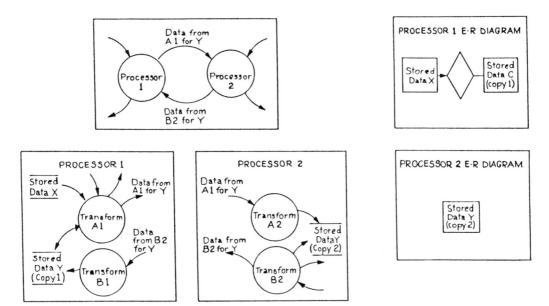

Figure 3.18 Duplication of stored data by one processor.

3.6 The mechanics of allocation

We recommend carrying out the allocation process by working top-down through the leveled essential model. At each level of the model, each transformation can be checked to see if it can be allocated to a single processor in its entirety. If so, the transformation can be "tagged" as belonging to that processor, and the lower levels of that transformation need not be examined further. If a lowest-level transformation is reached that cannot be allocated as a unit, the transformation must be split, as described in Section 3.4, and the pieces tagged appropriately.

After the transformations are allocated, the stored data should be allocated as described in Section 3.5. Stores and object types/relationships should be tagged for processor ownership. Any transformations that must be split because of data ownership decisions should be modified and tagged accordingly.

When the tagging is complete, the processor stage of the implementation model can be constructed. A screen storage area (or a sheet of paper if the transformation schemas are not stored in a development support machine) should be reserved for each candidate processor. The tagged portions of the essential model should then be copied into the areas for the processors, and joined along common flows and stores. The result of this procedure is a set of transformation schemas, one for each candidate processor.

3.7 Completing the processor stage of the implementation model

The transformation schemas created by the allocation procedure may now be integrated into a leveled model.

The upper levels of this model can be created by building a transformation schema with one transformation per processor. The input and output flows and stores for the transformations are the net inputs and outputs from the lower-level schemas. If there are a large number of processors, more than one higher level may be necessary, with some highest-level transformations representing groups of related processors.

The lower levels of the model are created by copying over the corresponding lower-level portions of the essential model (lower-level transformation schemas and transformation specifications).

Since the leveling scheme is different for the implementation model than it was for the essential model, the numbers assigned to transformations will differ between the two models. We recommend creating a cross-reference so that individual transformations can be traced from one model to another. This subject is treated in more detail in Chapter 12, Implementation Model Traceability.

It is important to verify that the processor stage of the implementation model is a complete and correct mapping of the essential model onto the processor configuration. One obvious mechanical verification is to check that all elements of the essential model have been assigned to one of the candidate processors. Another verification is to create a scenario for execution of the essential model, as described in Chapter 9 of Volume 1, Executing the Transformation Schema. A necessary condition for correctness of the implementation model is that execution of the scenario produce the same result as for the essential model.

3.8 Summary

The processor stage of the implementation model is created by reorganizing the content of the essential model to reflect the choice of a processor configuration. We have described the criteria for processor choice and the mechanics of the reorganization. Note that the portion of the essential model assigned to a processor has no special internal organization. We will take up this level of organization in the next chapter.

4
Task Modeling

4.1 Introduction

The processor model provides a specification of the transformations and stored data assigned to each processor used to implement a system. It is now necessary to reorganize and elaborate the model to adapt it to the *internal organization* of each processor. This step corresponds to the second stage of the implementation model — the task stage.

The processor model may prescribe the use of any type of processor, and thus portions of the model may be implemented not only as software but also as hard-wired circuits or even as manual procedures. Since we must now account for their internal organization, we must begin to distinguish between different types of processors. In this chapter, we shall focus our attention on programmable digital computers and thus on software implementations.

Each manufacturer of digital computers has developed its own vocabulary to describe the internal organization of the units of software within their processors, and there is therefore little standardization of the terminology. Since we shall be using some nomenclature that is in use elsewhere, it is important to distinguish between our general use of the term *task* and the specific use to which it is put on particular systems. We define a task as any named, independently schedulable piece of software that implements some portion of the transformation work assigned to a processor. Several vendors use the term more restrictively, for example to exclude software units like interrupt handlers.

In this chapter, we discuss the application of the implementation modeling heuristics to construct a model that describes the organization of software within digital computers.

4.2 The nature of tasks

The task is the basic unit of activity of a processor. We require that a lowest-level task be sequential, and thus concurrency is prohibited within the lowest level of tasks described by an implementation model. However, a group of potentially concurrent tasks can be aggregated into a single higher-level task. For the remainder of the chapter, we will use "task" to mean a lowest-level task unless otherwise noted. Tasks may be truly concurrent with each other if they run on different processors, or on a multi-processor capable of running several tasks simultaneously. In implementations that require more concurrent tasks than there are processors, a processor can *simulate* concurrency by switching between tasks so that an external observer is unable to distinguish the processor's behavior from several processors (or a multiprocessor) running concurrently.

Each task may be enabled or disabled, interrupted, and resumed. We define the terms enabled and disabled in the same way as when we discussed transformations in Chapter 6 of Volume 1 — Modeling Transformations. That is, when a task is enabled it is able to accept input and produce outputs, and when a task is disabled it cannot accept inputs nor produce outputs. From the point of view of a run-time operating system, a disabled task does not exist.

Real tasks take time, unlike transformations on the essential model. It is possible for a task to be interrupted and resumed after it has been enabled to allow other tasks to make use of execution resources. The system software of the processor will switch between several enabled tasks by interrupting one task and resuming another, often making choices in terms of a *priority* ordering for the tasks. The system software keeps data about the operation of the task, called the *context* of the task. When the system software is switching between one task and another, no useful application work is being done, but the processor is said to be *context switching*. The time it takes the processor to carry out this activity is the *context switching time*. The system software can manage the scheduling of tasks by allowing tasks to run while other tasks are waiting for completion of input/output operations by peripheral devices. Another management strategy is *time-slicing*, giving each task some fraction of the available time.

It is often useful to partition the "enabled" quality of a task into further distinguishing states of the task as follows:

- A task is *running* if it is currently in control of the execution resources within the processor and is actually performing transformation work.

- A task is *suspended* if it has data available for it to transform but presently is not in control of execution resources within the processor and is therefore between interruption and resumption.

- A process is *waiting for input* if it has relinquished control of the processor because it has no data to process, or is in an idle loop waiting for its data.

Please note that a task that executes a request for input or output but then continues to carry out useful work is *running*.

We now move on to describe how a portion of an implementation model to be implemented as software on a single processor may be allocated to a set of tasks.

4.3 Basic mechanics of task allocation

Chapter 3, Processor Modeling, described the first stage of implementation modeling as reorganizing the essential model around a set of candidate processors. Task modeling can be similarly described as a reorganization of portions of the essential model around a set of candidate tasks. The portions of the essential model referred to are those that were allocated to individual processors during the processor modeling stage.

An allocation to processors does not change the content of an essential model, but simply redistributes the content. Neither does processor allocation centralize control nor restrict any potential concurrency described by the essential model. The number of control transformations is at least as large as in the essential model, and any potentially concurrent transformation in the essential model remains potentially concurrent in the allocated model. The lack of restriction reflects the fact that concurrency and decentralized control can occur among a set of interacting processors, and also among a set of tasks within a multitasking processor.

Allocating portions of a model to a single task changes this situation, since control must be centralized and concurrency is prohibited within a (lowest-level) task. Task allocation will therefore involve modifications of the model to combine control transformations and their associated state diagrams, and to impose sequences on potentially concurrent data transformations.

Combining of a pair of state diagrams is the inverse of the procedure described in Section 3.4 of the last chapter:

Step 1. Add an "undefined" state to any state transition diagram that is enabled by another. Make the undefined state the initial state, and connect it to the transition to the original initial state with a condition of "enable." Add transitions from all other states to the undefined state with conditions of "disable" and actions to deactivate any transformations activated within the diagram.

Step 2. Begin a new state diagram by creating a state that combines the initial (constituent) states of the two original diagrams. This will be referred to as the *combined* state.

Step 3. For each condition external to both original diagrams and causing a transition from either of the constituent states and not already dealt with, construct a transition from the combined state and reproduce the condition and the actions from the original transition. Replace any action that sends an event flow to one of the original diagrams with the actions triggered by that event flow.

Step 4. If the external condition from Step 3 causes transitions in both original diagrams, construct a new combined state from the destination states of the original diagrams if distinct from all states already created, and draw the transition to it. Otherwise, construct a new combined state from the destination state of the original diagram with the transition and the current constituent state of the other original diagram, if distinct from all states already created, and draw the transition to it. If the destination state for the condition is a combined state created in an earlier step, draw the transition to it.

Step 5. Repeat steps 3 and 4 for any new combined state created in step 4.

Let's apply this procedure to an example drawn from the Cruise Control system essential model, Appendix A of Volume 2. Figure 4.1 shows a fragment of the preliminary transformation schema containing four control transformations; event flows to data transformations have been omitted to simplify the picture. The state-transition diagrams corresponding to transformations 1 and 2 are shown in Figures 4.2 and 4.3. Applying the combination procedure to these two diagrams has the following results:

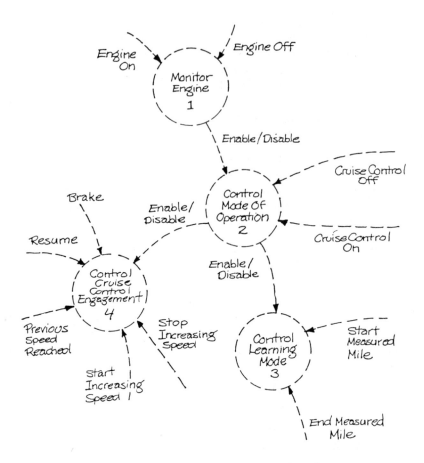

Figure 4.1 Fragment of preliminary transformation schema.

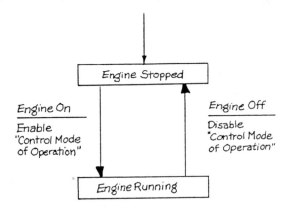

Figure 4.2 Monitor engine.

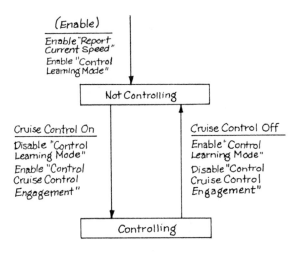

Figure 4.3 Control mode of operation.

Cycle 1. An "undefined" state called Precontrolling and associated transitions are added to Control Mode of Operation through application of step 1. The resulting diagram is shown in Figure 4.4. Step 2 requires the construction of a state called Engine Stopped/Precontrolling from the initial states of the two original diagrams. The only external condition causing a transition from one of the constituent states is Engine On from Engine Stopped; step 3 requires the corresponding action to be replaced by the action triggered in Control Mode of Operation. Since Engine On causes transitions in both original diagrams, step 4 causes a combined state called Engine Running/Not Controlling to which the transition is drawn. Figure 4.5 shows the new diagram up to this point.

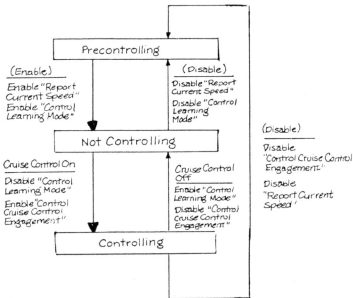

Figure 4.4 Result of applying step 1 to Figure 4.3

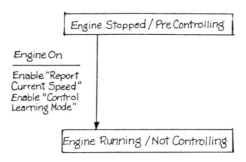

Figure 4.5 Combined diagram after cycle 1.

Cycle 2. We return to step 3 and apply the rules to the newly-created Engine Running/Not Controlling state. There are two external conditions from constituent states, Engine Off and Cruise Control On. Engine Off causes transitions in both diagrams and a corresponding replacement of actions. Cruise Control On causes a transition only in Control Mode of Operation. In step 4, Engine Off is seen to cause transitions to Precontrolling and Engine Stopped. Since this combination has already been included in the new diagram, the transition is connected to it. Cruise Control On, on the other hand, causes the creation of an Engine Running/Controlling state from a combination of a new destination state with one of the current constituent states, and the connection of the transition to this new state. Figure 4.6 shows the diagram at the end of cycle 2.

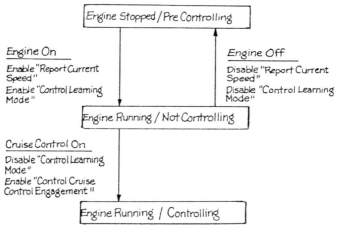

Figure 4.6 Combined diagram after cycle 2.

Cycle 3. There are two external conditions causing transitions from the constituents of the new state, namely Engine Off and Cruise Control Off. There are no new state combinations generated, and the results of this final cycle are shown in Figure 4.7. The diagram is consistent with an intuitive conception of the joint effect of the two original diagrams.

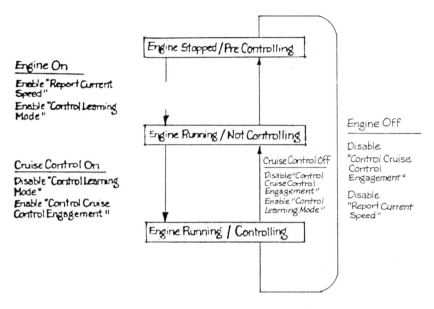

Figure 4.7 Final combined state transition diagram.

The reader is invited to refer to the state-transition diagram for Control Learning Mode (transformation 3 from Figure 4.1) in Appendix A of volume 2 and to combine it with the diagram of Figure 4.7. The results are shown in Figure 4.8. Note that the

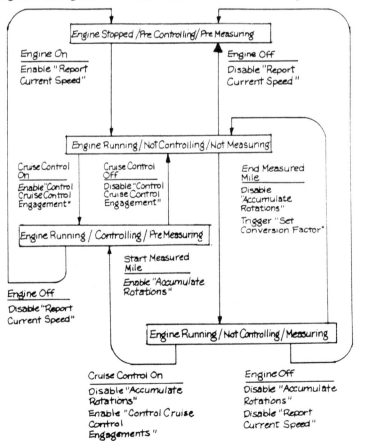

Figure 4.8 Combination of three state transition diagrams.

measured mile can be interrupted by turning the cruise control on. This is derivable from tracing the connections among the original three diagrams, but is more clearly seen in the combined diagram.

The procedure just described centralizes control but does not remove concurrency. State diagrams containing sections like that illustrated in Figure 4.9, in which two data transformations are concurrently enabled, can be allocated to a single task along with the data transformations. In order to ensure that the task is a true sequential process, the model of Figure 4.9 must be modified to prevent A and B from being simultaneously active. Such a modification is shown in general terms in Figure 4.10; the conditions causing transitions among the three states depend on the nature of A and B and will be discussed in later sections of this chapter. Note that the model of Figure 4.10 is not equivalent to the model of Figure 4.9. At best, the model of Figure 4.10 will satisfactorily simulate the model of Figure 4.9.

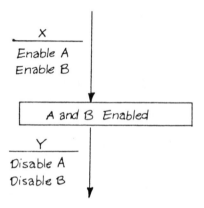

Figure 4.9 Concurrently enabled data transformations.

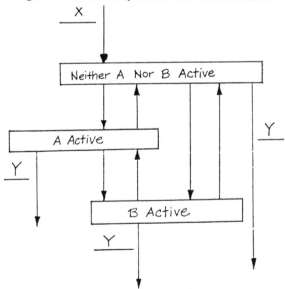

Figure 4.10 Sequential approximation of Figure 4.9.

The procedures illustrated in this section, centralization of control and removal of concurrency, underlie all the modeling transformations to be discussed in the remaining sections of this chapter.

4.4 Allocation of continuous transformations

An essential model may contain continuous flows and transformations that continuously transform those flows. In an implementation model, such transformations may be allocated to analog processors that are capable of carrying out truly continuous behavior. However, a digital computer may only run discrete tasks, and any continuously operating transformation allocated to a digital computer must be cast into implementable discrete tasks.

The technique is to allocate the continuously operating transformation to a task that runs periodically; the task *samples* the continuously available data, processes the data to produce outputs, and is then disabled, to be reenabled after a fixed interval. Any portion of the transformation that operates discretely, such as the computation of a setpoint, must be factored out and executed before the periodic process is activated. For example, Figure 4.11 shows two transformations from the Cruise Control System (Appendix A) that have been allocated to separate tasks. When the driver presses the Cruise Control On switch, the resultant interrupt causes a single activation of Record Rotation Rate, and initiates a periodic activation of Maintain Constant Speed to simulate continuous maintenance. The essential requirement will be satisfactorily approximated if the sampling interval is short enough to resolve the highest frequency variation in the input flow that must be detected [1]. The sampling rate, and therefore the interval, can be computed for each transformation by examining the environmental constraints — specifically, the frequency of variation in the input flow, the specification of the transformation, and the speed at which the external processes under control can respond.

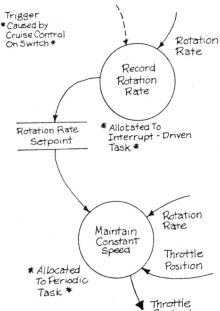

Figure 4.11 Continuous transformation factored into initializing and periodic components.

Each continuously operating transformation could now be allocated to a separate periodic task which runs at the rate necessary to satisfy the environmental constraints imposed on the essential transformation. However, limitations on the number of tasks that may be scheduled to run and the costs of context switching between tasks may lead to a need to group several essential transformations together into a single task. For example, three transformations with required sampling intervals of 40 ms, 50 ms, and 60 ms may all be classified together and allocated to a single task that operates on a 40 ms interval. While this arrangement carries out more processing than is required (the 50 ms and 60 ms fragments are running more frequently than needed), it is nevertheless often necessary since it may be impractical to allocate every transformation to a separate task.

When several concurrent transformations are allocated to a task, concurrency must be removed to accommodate the sequential nature of the task. Figure 4.12, derived from the Bottle-filling System (Appendix B), is a specialization of Figure 4.9 to deal with the issue of allocating continuous transformations. If the Control pH and Control Input Valve transformations are allocated to a single task, the control logic must be modified as shown by Figure 4.13. In this case, the control considerations are relatively simple. The code for performing the pH and input valve control loops can simply be sequenced inside the task. The remainder of the control can be implemented by scheduling the task to run at the necessary interval using the operating system scheduler or a timer, and an essential requirement to disable the transformation can be implemented by requesting the operating system to stop activating the task. The Enable and Disable statements in the essential model are simply replaced by calls to the operating system.

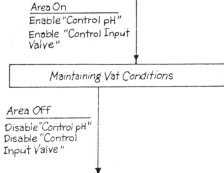

Figure 4.12 Concurrently enabled continuous transformations.

The situation becomes more complex when several continuous transformations are allocated to a single periodic task, and the enabling and disabling actions are asynchronous. Each transformation is to be enabled or disabled independently of other transformations allocated to the task; therefore, the control of the transformations cannot be implemented by enabling and disabling the entire task. The periodic task must be activated when the system is initialized, but component portions that correspond to disabled transformations must not run. The flags shown in Figure 4.14 represent control information that states whether each portion is to run. Please note that the control information is represented by a *data store*, not a control store. (A control store is an essential model variant of a semaphore mechanism.) A task that implements the control transformation is responsible for setting and resetting flags as an implementation of the enabling/disabling logic, as shown in Figure 4.14 drawn from the Cruise Control

System. Note that the Speed Control task contains transformations to maintain, increase, and resume speed. Which one is run during an activation is controlled by the flags.

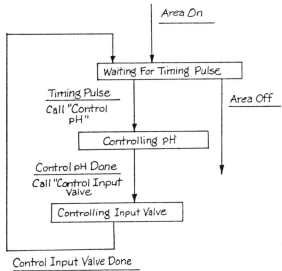

Figure 4.13 Sequential, discrete approximation of Figure 4.11.

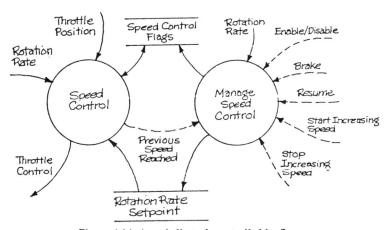

Figure 4.14 A periodic task controlled by flags.

Finally, please note that it is important to retain separation of control transformations from data transformations. Sometimes a continuous transformation that recognizes an event (say a critical temperature value) is allocated to the same periodic task as a continuous transformation (say one that maintains temperature) that is enabled or disabled by the event. If control of the overall state is entrusted to another task, the event recognizer should signal the control task, which in turn will set the appropriate flags. Failure to centralize controlling decisions is an invitation to the introduction of timing problems.

Each of the continuously operating transformations on the processor model may now be allocated to tasks to produce the task model. Several factors affect the choice of tasks:

- the number of tasks that may be simultaneously enabled is often limited;

- context switching between tasks costs time and execution resources;

- the memory usage of a task may be limited;

- each task is discrete and can only do one thing at a time.

Consider a collection of continuously operating transformations that must operate at no more than 10 ms, 12 ms, 15 ms, 20 ms, and 35 ms intervals, with a system software organization that is severely limited in the number of tasks it can run simultaneously. A simple solution is to run all the transformations in sequence every 10 ms. This can be a satisfactory approximation of the essential model if the implementation constraints are met, although it wastes execution resources since the 35 ms. transformation is running more often than necessary. Two common failures of this simple solution are, first, that the task takes too long to run, and second, that the task occupies too much memory. We shall examine some variations of the solution that can avoid these failures.

First, if the task takes too long to run, we must take advantage of the fact that not all transformations need to be run every 10 ms; we could, for example, run the task every 5 ms, offsetting the lower-sampling rate transformations by multiples of 5 ms as shown in Table 4.1. The task must keep a count of the pulse number, and run the appropriate transformation only when necessary. (This solution assumes that the first three transformations collectively take less than 5 ms, and each of the last two take less than 5 ms each.) An alternative representation for this organization is a time line, as shown in Figure 4.15. The table, the time line, or an equivalent state diagram specify a control transformation that activates the enabled transformations within the periodic task and that must be modeled in addition to the control transformation that controls the enabling and disabling of the data transformations allocated to the periodic task.

Transformation		Interval In Pulses	Offset	Pulse Number											
				0	1	2	3	4	5	6	7	8	9	10
A	10ms	2 (10ms)	0	X		X		X		X		X		X
B	12ms	2 (10ms)	0	X		X		X		X		X		X
C	15ms	2 (10ms)	0	X		X		X		X		X		X
D	20ms	4 (20ms)	1		X				X				X	
E	35ms	4 (20ms)	3				X				X			

Table 4.1 Sampling rate table.

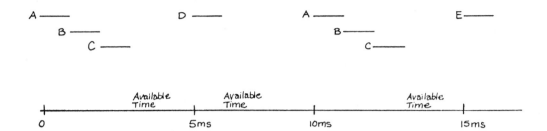

Figure 4.15 A time line.

Second, if the task uses too much memory, it must be split into two pieces: one that runs every 10 ms and another than runs every 20 ms, for example. The resulting tasks may either be run offset from one another, say, every 5 ms as shown in Figure 4.16, or they may run at different priorities. This second solution may introduce data consistency problems if the two tasks share data since they may be attempting to modify the same data within the same time interval; a useful technique is to copy shared data into the receiving task at the beginning of each pulse.

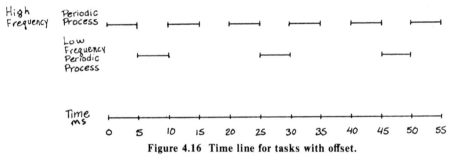

Figure 4.16 Time line for tasks with offset.

In a system software organization that permits many tasks to be enabled simultaneously, these complications need not arise since each transformation can be assigned to a separate task. (However, the use of any shared data must be synchronized by spacing out when the tasks run, or by copying the data as described above). In this case, a time line or an equivalent state diagram can act as a specification for a control transformation embodied in the system software for controlling the processor, and it should be supplied as an overall specification for the task level of the implementation model. The details of modeling application-specific aspects of system software are described in Chapter 6 — Modeling System Services — Process Management.

4.5 Allocation of discrete transformations

Tasks that incorporate transformations of discrete data must run when the data becomes available. In the previous section, we examined tasks containing transformations of continuous flows in which we *chose* the rate at which the task was to run, subject to environmental constraints. Here, we do not have the same flexibility, but the principles remain the same: we must satisfactorily approximate the behavior of the essential model with minimum distortion.

In the perfect world of the essential model, we assumed that transformations completed their activities instantaneously; clearly, this does not match the reality. The processing time taken to produce the outputs from inputs must be within the bounds specified by the corresponding constraint; this depends on the speed of access to stored data and the amount of work to be done.

We can have an adequate implementation of a discrete transformation, if the time needed to process an input is within response time constraints, and either:

- the inputs can be guaranteed to arrive at intervals longer than the time needed to process an input, or

- the *average* interval between the arrival of inputs is less than the average time needed to process an input, *and* either a queuing mechanism for the data or multiple copies of the task are provided.

If the first condition is met, a task containing discrete transformations executes until it requires input, at which point it must idle or pass control back to the processor and enter the waiting for input state. When the input arrives, the task can resume running. Typically, a task of this type will execute a *read* that sets in motion the activities necessary to get the data. Alternatively the task may idle until the system software sets a flag indicating that data is present.

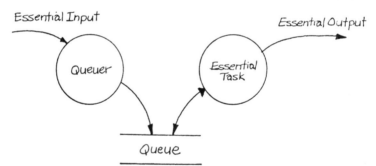

Figure 4.17 Queuer for essential input.

If the data may at times arrive more rapidly than the task can transform the data, then a queuing mechanism can be introduced as shown in Figure 4.17. The addition of a queuing mechanism accomplishes the transformation with two tasks: the *essential task* (that which actually transforms the data) and an intermediate task that queues the arriving inputs, a *queuing task*. The control aspects of this model are as follows:

- The queuer is initially enabled and a read is executed; the queuer is then in the waiting for input state. When input arrives it is queued; the queuer loops, executes a read, and again enters the waiting for input state.

- The essential task is initially enabled, and a read is executed, and the task is now waiting for input. When the queuer notifies the operating system that data is available in the queue, then the essential activity may execute. In the meantime, another input may arrive: the essential task is suspended, the queuer executes, then the essential task continues processing the previous input. When the first input is completely processed another read is executed; if an item is available, execution on that input may begin, otherwise the essential task once again is waiting for input.

Please note that this scheme is limited by three factors. First, if data arrives faster than the queuer can queue the data then the scheme cannot work. Second, if the queue can hold n data items, and n + 1 items arrive within a time shorter than that required to transform a single item, then the queue will fill up and data will be lost. This situation represents a burst of data that cannot be processed with a chosen queue size; the *burst rate* for inputs handled in this manner should be computed to set the queue size. Third, the delay between the arrival of the data and the production of the output must be within the required response time.

The introduction of the queuing task on the input flow allows the essential transformation to be carried out correctly with less sensitivity to the arrival rates of input data. The advantage of creating the queuer as a separate task to handle the arrival of discrete data inputs is simply that the distortion of the essential model is minimized. Save the fact that the essential task reads a queue rather than the data directly, the fragment is the same as the essential model from which it is derived. Another way of stating the same thing is to say that the implementation technology is *transparent* to the application code that implements the essential task.

4.6 Summary

Task allocation is an activity similar to processor allocation in that it involves reorganization around a set of chosen implementation units. However, the requirements that tasks be sequential, have centralized control, operate discretely, match data arrival rates, and maintain stored data integrity, may require substantial modifications to the model used as input to the allocation. The nature of these modifications, and the implications of the corresponding implementation choices, have been examined in this chapter. In the next chapter, we will focus on the modeling of interfaces within an implementation model.

Chapter 4: References

1.   "Nyquist Frequency" in Van Nostrand's Scientific Encyclopedia, 5th edition. New York, Van Nostrand Reinhold Company, 1976.

5
Interface Modeling

5.1 Introduction

The allocation of transformations to processors and tasks tends to fragment the transformations and to introduce additional inter-processor and inter-task data flows and stores. The interfaces between processors and tasks must therefore be examined for potential problems involving data exchange, stored data access, and control synchronization. In addition, the communication represented by the flows may be elaborated for three reasons. First, the essential model idealization of modeling only net flow of data must now be dropped, and the full set of connections shown. Second, in addition to the content of the data that is communicated it is also necessary to model the *form* of the data, particularly that presented to a human being, such as an operator. Third, if inter-task flows must be sequenced, there are cooperating control interactions between the tasks that must be modeled. Typically, several essential model fragments are allocated to a pair of communicating tasks in the implementation model. These tasks can only transmit or receive one chunk of data at a time, and control is therefore required for each task to model the communication.

Please note that in this chapter we will deal with the dynamics of the interface only from the application's point of view. We will thus be focusing on inter-task interfaces independently of whether the tasks are in the same or different processors. Aspects of interface operation that can be carried out by system utilities in a "transparent" manner, such as the details of a graphics service or a task communication manager, will be discussed in the next chapter.

5.2 Synchronization of data flow

In Section 4.5 of Chapter 4, an intermediate queuing task was interposed between an input and the task that transformed it. The control of the two tasks was described in detail to show how sensitivity to input flow arrival rate could be reduced, as is sometimes necessary to allow an implementation to meet constraints. We now turn to the general problem of synchronizing the data flow between two tasks, and show that the queuing task is a special case of a general solution.

Consider two tasks that communicate via a data flow Y as shown in Figure 5.1. Both tasks are assumed to have the same priority, and, for simplicity, we shall initially assume that each task completes work on a single packet of input data before the other task is allowed to run. To understand the implementation of the inter-task data movement, recall that a discrete flow consists of two components: the data itself, and an associated trigger that signals the presence of the data. Figure 5.2 shows an elaboration of Figure 5.1 to add the flow of control, and Figure 5.3 shows a state transition diagram that specifies Control Supplier. (In a well-designed implementation, both Control Supplier and Control Consumer would normally reside in the operating system and would be generalized to handle any pair of communicating tasks.)

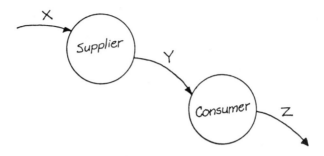

Figure 5.1 Two communicating tasks.

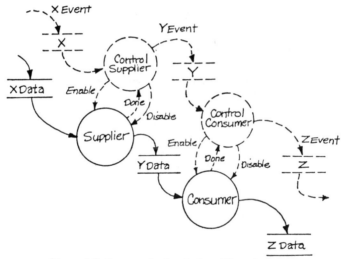

Figure 5.2 Communicating tasks with control.

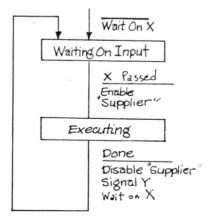

Figure 5.3 Specification for control supplier.

If we make the additional assumptions that the data stores shown in Figure 5.2 act as first-in-last-out queues with infinite capacity, and that the Supplier and Consumer transformations take a finite amount of time to operate, it is possible to extend the execution rules in Chapter 9 of Volume 1, Executing the Transformation Schema, to cover the execution of Figures 5.2 and 5.3. Let us modify the execution rules so that each time a data transformation operates, the execution halts and the token placement is reexamined before another execution step begins. It will also be permissible to make additional token placements while an execution step is taking place; tokens are placed on event flows only. This will allow us to simulate the effects of data arriving during the execution of a transformation.

Notice that we have not imposed the requirement that the Supplier and Consumer transformations operate in alternation. Since the effect of simultaneous token presence is sequential execution in indeterminate order, it is possible that the Supplier operates several times in succession even though tokens are available that would cause the consumer to be activated. However, the Consumer will eventually be activated to accept each piece of data sent by the Supplier. Also, if the Consumer operates many times in succession, it will ultimately run out of tokens and force the Supplier to be selected. Thus, although there may be indefinite time delays, there are no synchronization problems introduced by the control scheme. The control aspects of the synchronization are completely transparent to the Supplier and Consumer transformations, which simply run when they are activated. As we will discuss in Chapter 6, Modeling System Services — Process Management, the synchronization control need not be incorporated into the implementation model.

This philosophy of task synchronization can be extended to cover the general case of a set of tasks that transform a stream of data. Consider a set of tasks as shown in Figure 5.4; each packet of data (shown by a filled-in square) can be processed concurrently and independently with no synchronization problems.

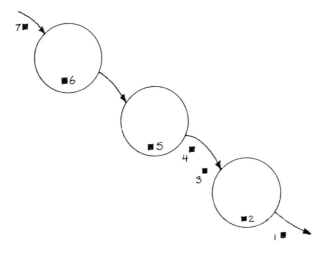

Figure 5.4 Concurrent tasks with data stream.

This philosophy requires that the system software manage the synchronization of the data flow; the control from the point of view of the essential model is simply to enable *all* the tasks — the tasks downstream simply wait for input to be produced as output by those tasks upstream. This can then guarantee that there are no synchronization problems either from the point of view of the implementation or of the essential model. UNIX® employs this scheme as a development environment, and real-time versions of the operating system are also available.

Similar techniques can also be used when several streams of data require independent but synchronized processing as shown in Figure 5.5. In this case, the tasks after X and before Y can be concurrently running in parallel with each other. The simplicity of this scheme can be visualized if the task marked S is a sort that requires all its input before any output can be produced. While S is gathering data the tasks that do not depend on S for input can run independently. Input can queue up in front of Y until S and its downstream task produce data.

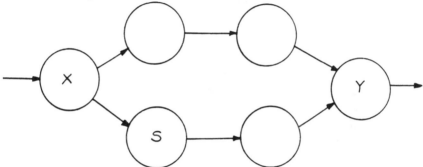

Figure 5.5 Parallel tasks requiring synchronization.

Let us now reexamine some of the simplifying assumptions that were made regarding Figures 5.3 and 5.4. First, we assumed that each data-transforming task completed operation before the other was allowed to operate. Since the only connection between Supplier and Consumer is the queue (as mediated by the control embodied in the operating system), the only fundamental requirement is that the reading and writing of the smallest transferrable data unit to or from the queue, once initiated, is uninterruptable. This will prevent loss of data on transfers to or from the queue. Second, we assumed that both data-transforming tasks had equal priority. The only fundamental requirement is that the combination of arrival rate and priority does not cause the Supplier task to be invariably selected at the end of an execution step. If this requirement and the requirement of uninterruptable data transfer are met, it is even permissible for one task to preempt the other during execution.

5.3 Synchronization of access to stored data

In Section 5 of Chapter 4, stored data was seen as an implementation of a queuing mechanism for managing the rapid arrival and processing of discrete data units. Synchronization on the stored data was effected by the system software, using the fact that the two cooperating tasks could never access the same unit of data. (Since the data items are organized into a queue, the consumer task will always take a unit of data previously placed by the supplier; the case that there is only one element is handled by the supplier having a higher priority than the consumer or by making access to the element uninterruptible.) We now consider the synchronization of several transformations accessing stored data in a non-queuing situation.

The basis of stored data access synchronization problems is that the transformations that access the store are asynchronous with respect to one another. Once we assume that the tasks that carry out the transformations take time, it is possible for a task to attempt to read data which has not yet been written by some other task. There are several approaches to this problem; the one chosen will affect the choice of tasks and allocation to them.

First, the problem can be ignored. Consider two continuously operating transformations approximated by two tasks at two different sampling rates. Assuming, of course, that the tasks share data, it is possible for one task to interrupt the other during the act of writing several related data items. The consumer process will then read some data items from sample t_{i-1} and some from sample t_i. We can ignore this difference if i-1 values are a reasonable approximation to i values.

Second, sensitive data can be copied as a unit. The highest priority task should always be responsible for the copying, since this can guarantee that the task will not be interrupted by another user of the data. The producer of the data, however, should be in control of the activation of the copying. Consider Figure 5.6, in which both temperature and pressure must be ramped simultaneously when set to new setpoints by the operator. (It is assumed that a one cycle disparity between the two values is an unsatisfactory approximation.) The store containing the copy flag is read each cycle by the Control Reaction task; if the flag is set, *both* setpoints are copied from modifiable to active storage, and the flag is reset. The task Store New Setpoint will only set the flag when both of the setpoints have been set. This method, of course, only applies when the high-priority task can operate effectively on the previous data while new data is being entered.

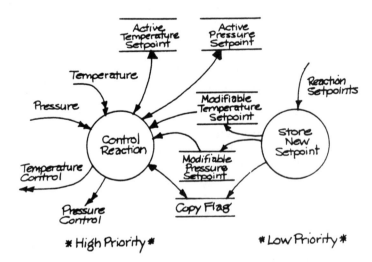

Figure 5.6 Copying shared stored data.

Third, the task can be made uninterruptable. Consider two tasks that write common data items that operate at the same priority; if the system software should choose to interrupt one of the tasks when the items have been only partially written, inconsistent data will result. The solution here is to make the writing of the data an atomic operation by making the section of the code that writes the data items uninterruptible. If this is impractical, a flag may be used to lock the data items. All tasks that share the data must test the flag before using the data. The reset and set operations must be atomic operations — indivisible and uninterruptible. This can be implemented via a semaphore [1].

Fourth, the data may be protected by an intermediate task, a "data server." Requests to read and write data are given to a task that "owns" the data. Since the task can, by definition, carry out only one operation at a time, each operation on the data can be guaranteed to be atomic.

5.4 Synchronization of control

Each control transformation that does not communicate with other control transformations may be allocated to a single task without synchronization problems. Consider the task a containing a control transformation and the tasks containing its controlled data transformations as a group. The entire group of tasks is free of synchronization problems; each task that implements a data transformation is enabled/disabled by the control transformation, and runs when data is made available or when it is requested to run. Interrupts and resumes carried out by system software are transparent to these tasks as described in Section 5 of the previous chapter. Similarly, the task that implements the control transformation may only operate on a single event flow at once; simultaneously arriving event flows are processed in indeterminate order just as defined by the essential model.

When two control tasks communicate, however, synchronization problems can arise. In Figure 5.7 for example, the task A emits an event flow R when P occurs.

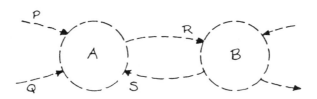

Figure 5.7 Two communicating control transformations.

Depending on the state of task B, an S event flow may or may not be produced, and task A responds differently to a subsequent Q depending on whether an intervening S has been received as shown in Figure 5.8.

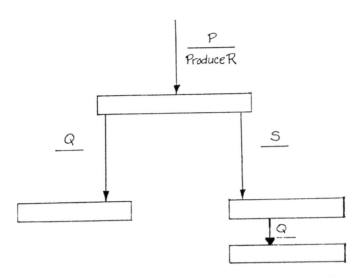

Figure 5.8 Partial state transition diagram for transformation A from Figure 5.7.

In the essential model idealization, the arrival of a flow instantaneously triggers *all* of the transformations that operate on that flow and all subsequent transformations with direct flow connections to the first. (See Chapter 9, Volume 1, Executing the Transformation Schema.) In an implementation, however, the B task may be suspended to allow task A to run, and task A may therefore respond to an intervening Q event flow before it can receive an S. We now have a possible synchronization problem.

Three solutions are possible. First, the B task may be run with a higher priority if it must *always* finish its activities before task A runs. This may not be possible if the S event flow then causes another event flow to be produced that must then be completely processed — possibly by task B! Second, the control transformation specifications may be modified to send and receive positive confirmations of the communicating event flows. In the example of Figure 5.7, we would have to add a control store for Q and an event flow from task B whose interpretation is "there is no S" as shown in Figure 5.9 and modify the specification as shown in Figure 5.10. The addition of the extra state requires that a control store be used for the Q event flow since it may arrive *before* the process has received the event flow from B. Third, the control transformations may be combined into a single task that, by definition, can do only one thing at a time. This may be cumbersome; but it is possible rigorously to construct the overall control transformation specification from descriptions of each of the original control transformations as described in Section 4.3 of the previous chapter.

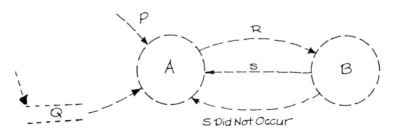

Figure 5.9 Modified schema to remove potential synchronization problem.

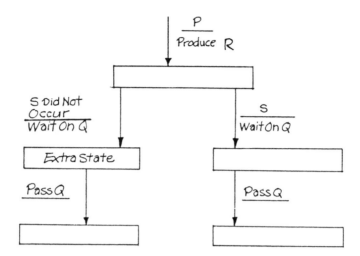

Figure 5.10 Modified partial state transition diagram for Transformation A from Figure 5.9.

5.5 Net flow of data and interfaces

On the context schema for the essential model, net flow of data is shown between terminators and the system. As implementation modeling proceeds a transformation is often divided between two tasks, one that carries out the system response and another that transforms the (net) essential flow from the terminator into components, as shown in Figure 5.11. In this illustration, drawn from the SILLY system (Appendix C in Volume 2), the transfer of a trigger word involves the selection of the "menu" mode, the manipulation of a cursor, and the choice of an entry format (binary or hexadecimal). The operator acts both as the source of the data and as the implementer of the data entry procedure.

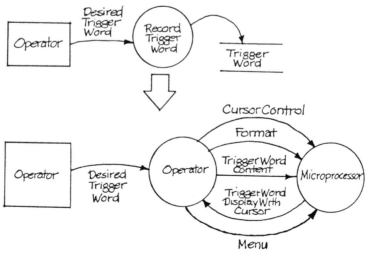

Figure 5.11 Elaboration of net flow.

Strictly speaking, *both* portions of the transformation carry out the system response; the original flow from the terminator may be thought of as the *idea* of the trigger word in the operator's mind. An interface model such as that shown in Figure 5.11 guarantees that the implementation model balances visually with the essential model; such a model is also important if the developers are responsible for defining the processing for both portions of the transformation. However, one can also view the task that transforms the flow into components as being carried out in the terminator. This results in the Operator task being subsumed within the Operator terminator rather than being separated out as in Figure 5.11. The operator's data entry procedure (or more generally, the "outer" portion of the allocated transformation), need not be defined and the data specification entry for Desired Trigger Word can be redefined to be made up of the components. Figure 5.12 shows the resulting model.

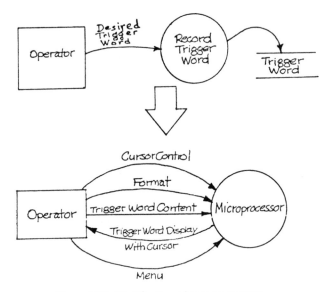

Figure 5.12 Modification of system context.

5.6 Interface dialogue flow specification

Any set of flows that constitutes a single unit of interaction we shall define as an *interface dialogue,* and model as a bidirectional flow with a single name as shown in Figure 5.13. The unit of interaction may be complex, containing a number of flows as in Figure 5.12. As another example, an interaction that causes statistics on the percentages of good and bad sheets on a particular inspection surface to be displayed constitutes an interface dialogue for the Defect Inspection System (Appendix D); it may consist of a prompt, a data entry screen for the inspection surface number, and so on.

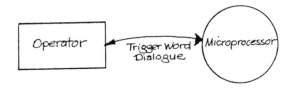

Figure 5.13 An interface dialogue flow.

As with all flows, an interface dialogue flow needs a data specification. The standard data specification syntax should be employed, together with an additional symbol (a colon, ':') to distinguish between the two directions of flow. The flow should be defined from the point of view of the *initiator;* the set of flows placed on the left of the separator should contain the flow that initiates the dialogue. A dialogue definition for Figure 5.13 is:

Trigger Word Dialogue = [Menu | Cursor Control | Format | Trigger Word Content]:
                      Trigger Word Display with Cursor

The data specification should *not* be used to specify *sequences* of stimuli or responses; that is properly the job of a control transformation and its associated specification.

The data specification may also be used to reference documents that define the form of data. A flow named Inspection Surface Statistics Screen, for example, may reference a layout of the screen to be built that is associated with the model (Figure 5.14). A screen may be defined by providing a generalized template, which prescribes standards for field placement, use of function keys, and so on. Alternatively, a specific screen layout can be created as in Figure 5.14. The medium of presentation of a screen layout has significant impact on the reviewability of the model. Screens rather than paper are obviously preferred; in this way there is no dissonance between the medium of the model and the actual medium to be used in the implementation.

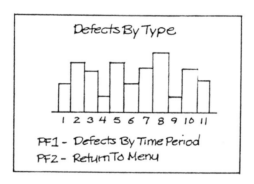

Figure 5.14 Screen layout example.

As with all system models, these screen layouts may be viewed as *prototypes.* To make the model still more effective, the passive presentation of the screen may be replaced by a more active representation in which stimuli can generate responses. Even if the responses produced are unrealistic in terms of the real world being monitored and controlled, this technique is most helpful in providing a "feel" of the interface to a prospective user.

Please note that the prototype is very unlikely to be usable as a component of an implemented system. The technology used to construct the prototype will be oriented to ease of modification of the screens, rather than to the stringent timing constraints typical of most real-time systems.

5.7 Modeling control of dialogues

The technique for modeling dialogue controls is to add a control transformation to each end of each dialogue; together, the control transformations manage the movement of data and control signals across the interface. The two control transformations must cooperate so that an action taken at one end of the dialogue causes a condition to be recognized at the other, which then takes an action, which may in turn cause a condition to be recognized, and so on. Figure 5.15 illustrates this interaction.

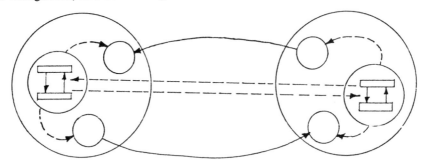

Figure 5.15 Management of dialogue by control transformations.

This abstract model may be implemented by packaging the control transformation and the data transformations that implement the actions into a single task. Control may be implemented by having each data transformation implemented as a subroutine, and the control transformation implemented as the high-level calling logic. Alternatively each transformation may be a separate task; the task that implements the control transformation recognizes conditions and employs the system software to activate and deactivate the other tasks.

The techniques of dialogue modeling can be applied to modeling control of device handlers. The task that implements the device handler enters into a cooperating set of activities with the device itself. The control transformation specification for the device (if it were modeled) must cooperate with that of the device handler task. The same situation applies for processor-to-processor communication facilities such as networks. In fact, many network protocols are specified with heavy emphasis on the control aspects of the cooperation between the processors, for example, the X25 protocol specification [2].

5.8 Use of services

There is no direct implementation of flows, in the sense that we can simply assign a flow to some piece of the implementation technology. Data and control signals move around in systems, certainly, but have to be moved by something active. The transformation schema uses the flow symbol to represent both the content and the movement of data and control. The active mechanism that moves the data or control is a *service*. The service mediates the interfaces between the implementation units on the model.

Services hide the details of transfers across interfaces. A high-level-language program reads data from a disk file oblivious to the complexities involved in moving the disk head to the correct cylinder of a disk, waiting for the correct sector, and then reading the data. The program is unaware of the sector organization and sizes. Similarly, tasks that use a graphics interface should be unaware of the details of the graphics system being used. The application is completely described by specifying the content and form of the interface together with the time sequencing of signals that cross the interface.

Whenever a service is transparent to the application, it *should not be modeled on the application model,* but separately on a different model, with an entirely different vocabulary. The service is a new subproblem; it is a piece of implementation technology that requires independent analysis. The fact that the implementation for an application uses several processors may be a justification for a network. This is not a requirement of the initial application problem, but it is derived from the chosen design. For example, we may need a graphics system that transfers data to and from a special-purpose screen. This represents the construction of a new piece of implementation technology, as a portion of the application project. However, there is no fundamental semantic connection between the application and the service: the service should know nothing about the application itself. The graphics system, in fact, should be independent enough to be used in an entirely different application. (This lack of a semantic connection between the application and the service poses some interesting modeling problems that we shall address in the next chapter.)

5.9 Summary

Interfaces should be modeled from the point of view of the application. The form and content of each interface should be defined in the data specification. The sequencing and control of data that crosses the interface may be modeled using two interlocked control transformations and their associated data transformations.

Chapter 5: References

1. Dijkstra, E.W., "Cooperating Sequential Processes," *Programming Languages,* ed. F. Genuys (New York: Academic Press, 1968).

2. Davies, D.W., et al. *Computer Networks and Their Protocols.* New York John Wiley & Sons, 1979.

6
Modeling System Services
— Process Management

6.1 Introduction

Many embedded systems have suffered from inflexibility. Accommodating a change in user requirements, or re-implementation in a new hardware or software environment, requires such extensive changes in these systems that they must be rebuilt from scratch. A major cause of inflexibility is failure to separate the portions of a system that implement the application from the portions that provide the support environment. The inflexibility of many early real-time systems was inevitable because of the limitations of the available processor hardware; maintainability can take precedence over operational efficiency only when there is sufficient capacity available. However, we have argued in Chapter 1 of Volume 1 that there is a large class of systems for which processor capacity *is* sufficient. Thus the problem-dominated approach to systems development dictates the separation of systems support from the application.

In this chapter, we will provide guidelines for identifying and modeling the system support environment required for an application. The scope of this chapter includes utilities such as device handlers, intertask or interprocessor communication managers, interrupt handlers, task dispatching routines, and mathematical subroutines. Utilities that primarily deal with the management, storage, and retrieval of stored data within a system, such as data base managers, are the subject of the next chapter.

6.2 Semantic levels

We define the *semantic level* as that combination of scope, boundary choices, and vocabulary that defines the modeler's point of view of a system. Please refer to the informal discussions of the banking system in Chapter 1 of Volume 1, which provides some preliminary examples. Let's return to the banking system and consider three tasks that might be included in an implementation:

- a task that receives a message packet sent over a data communications line, strips the parity bits, checks parity, and requests retransmission if necessary.

- a task that translates an ASCII character stream by identifying field markers and changing alphanumeric fields to EBCDIC format and numeric fields to fixed decimal format.

- a task that accepts a checking account deposit, checks it for legitimacy against a file of checking accounts, updates the file if the deposit is legitimate, and issues an audit report.

The three tasks are illustrated in Figure 6.1. Notice that the tasks are drawn in a disconnected fashion, although a banking transaction might well go through the three tasks in sequence. The problem is that the three tasks have different semantic levels, and thus have incompatible data flows. In order to connect the three tasks into a sequence, it is necessary to associate the semantic levels in some way. Figure 6.2 accomplishes this by mixing the semantic levels. The problem with this model is that it invites mixing application code and software support and pushes the system builder toward an inflexible design. Figure 6.3 provides another strategy for sequencing by defining all three tasks in a very abstract manner. Although the problem of mixed semantic levels has been avoided, all information about the primary semantic level (banking) has been lost.

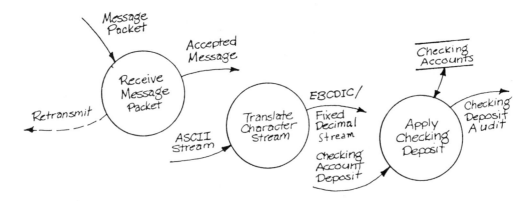

Figure 6.1 Three tasks with different semantic levels.

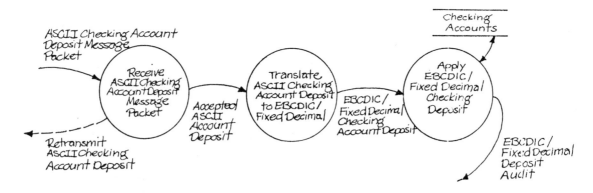

Figure 6.2 Three tasks with mixed semantic levels.

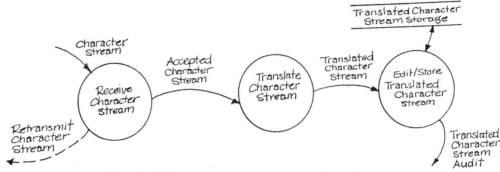

Figure 6.3 Three tasks at an abstract semantic level.

The problem illustrated by Figures 6.1, 6.2, and 6.3 occurs in a large number of implementation situations. To create a rigorous model of the implementation, it is necessary to describe the connection between the application tasks and the system utility tasks. However, a simple joining of models is not satisfactory for this purpose. Our solution is to build separate models for system utililties and to cross-reference them to the application model. The details of this solution will be laid out in the remaining sections of this chapter.

6.3 Essential models for system utilities

There are many cases when a formal model of a system utility is necessary for effective systems development. If a new utility must be built to support an application, a model is as important as in any other development situation. If an existing utility is reasonably complex, a model may be necessary to verify that the utility will interface satisfactorily to the application tasks. (If a model of a complex system utility doesn't exist, one may have to be created after the fact; reading code is not a very satisfactory way to visualize a system's operation.)

In most senses, a model of a system utility is no different from any other model. It can be built using the modeling tools and heuristics described in the present three volumes. In fact, a system utility built as an end in itself (say, as a product of a software house) is equivalent in all respects to an "application system." A system utility built as an offshoot of another development project has two characteristic differences from other development models. First, it is developed with a semantic level that is "referred to" by another semantic level. Although details of the original application are not included in the utility model, the appropriateness of the utility model will be judged partially by how conveniently it supports the application. Second, the semantic level of the utility model may be difficult to pin down because of its remoteness from the original application.

Let's explore a system utility that will be needed to implement the SILLY system (Appendix C in Volume 2) — a keyboard handler. The utility could be implemented as a hard-wired digital circuit. However, for now we'll just examine the essential model. The keyboard mechanism linked to the utility consists of a two-dimensional grid of read and write lines like the one illustrated by Figure 1.4 of Chapter 1 in Volume 2, Essential Modeling Heuristics. The context schema for the utility is shown in Figure 6.4. Note that there are no discrete input flows. The system is inherently time-driven and is based on four time intervals. The shortest time interval reflects the time required for the read line values to settle after the write line has been changed. The intermediate time intervals control the delay between the sending of the Key Available event flow and the actual key data, and the cycling of activation of the write lines. The longer interval drives the interpretation of accumulated line values (debouncing) to determine if an unambiguous hit has occurred. The external events for the system are Time to Cycle Write Lines, Time to Store Read Lines, Time to Check for Key Hit, and Time to Transmit.

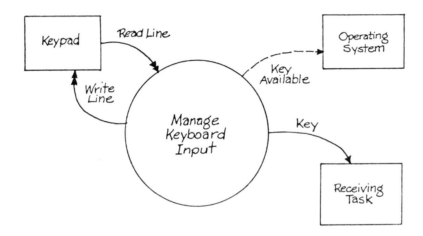

Figure 6.4 Keyboard handler context diagram.

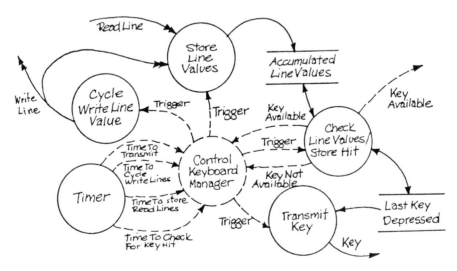

Figure 6.5 Manage keyboard input.

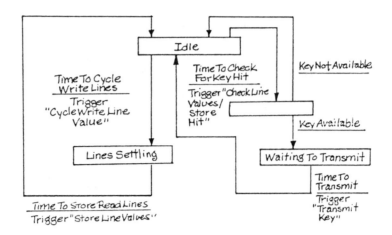

Figure 6.6 Control keyboard manager.

Figure 6.5 shows the transformation schema for the keyboard utility, and Figure 6.6 shows the state transition for the control transformation of Figure 6.5. The transformation specifications are:

Cycle Write Line Value

Precondition

WRITE LINE n high and all other WRITE LINEs low

Postcondition

WRITE LINE n+1 mod number of WRITE LINES high, and all other WRITE LINES low

Store Line Values

Precondition

None

Postcondition

WRITE LINE number of WRITE LINE with high value, and values of all READ LINEs added to ACCUMULATED LINE VALUES

Check Line Values/Store Hit

Local term: NULL ENTRY is a WRITE LINE number with all READ LINE values low

Local term: AMBIGUOUS ENTRY is a WRITE LINE number with two or more READ LINE values high

Precondition 1

> Most common entry in ACCUMULATED LINE VALUES
> is not NULL ENTRY and not AMBIGUOUS ENTRY

and   KEY associated with most common entry does not match
LAST KEY DEPRESSED

Postcondition 1

> KEY associated with most common entry is stored in LAST KEY DEPRESSED

and   ACCUMULATED LINE VALUES is empty

and   KEY AVAILABLE has been issued

Precondition 2

> not precondition 1

Postcondition 2

> KEY associated with most common entry is stored in LAST KEY DEPRESSED

and   ACCUMULATED LINE VALUES is empty

Notice that the model just presented is completely non-specific to the SILLY system — it will work with any application that requires keyboard input. The keyboard management system has its own specific semantic level, expressed here in terms of the structural details of the model and in terms of the naming of model elements.

If an implementation environment is reasonably complex, it may be necessary to define system utilities recursively. In other words, in order to implement a utility successfully, a second utility with a different semantic level might have to be defined. The second utility bears the same relationship to the first as the first does to the original application — the relation of providing a support environment. The levels of the ISO network architecture protocol [1] bear this relationship to one another, with each lower layer acting as a support environment for the upper layers.

6.4 Types of system utilities

System utilities may be categorized in terms of the relationship they bear to the essential model for which they provide support. The categories are:

- *interface utilities* that enable the data and control signals described by the essential model to be sent and received in a particular implementation environment,

- *transformation utilities* that actually carry out some of the work described by the essential model, and

- *control utilities* that manage the dynamics of the essential model transformations.

A fourth type of utility, one that provides the interface between the essential model transformations and the system's stored data, will be considered in detail in the next chapter.

Interface utilities are chosen to provide a buffer between the essential model and the details of sensor/actor technology, communication links such as data entry or display mechanisms, and the like. Interface utilities often constitute what Britton, Parker, and Parnas [2] have called a *virtual device*. In the ideal case, the utilities permit the application code to be written as though the simplest conceptual picture of the system inputs and outputs (that is, the essential model view) could be implemented directly.

Let's return to the job of making keyboard input from the SILLY system operator available to the application tasks. A utility to manage the keyboard mechanism and to send a data representation of the key that was depressed was described in Section 3 of this chapter. We will assume that the keyboard manager is implemented by a dedicated digital circuit, and that the digital circuit is interfaced to a processor that contains the SILLY application tasks. The interface to the processor consists of the Key Available signal, which acts as an interrupt, and the Key data, which is sent through a data line. Figure 6.7 illustrates the connections. The application task may be thought of as waiting for a command. When the keyboard manager interrupts, the operating system saves the environment of the application task and transfers control to a data line handler that receives and stores the data from the data line. When the data line handler is finished, the operating system restores the environment of the application task and reactivates it. The entire mechanism is invisible to the application task, which, when reactivated, finds that a command has suddenly appeared.

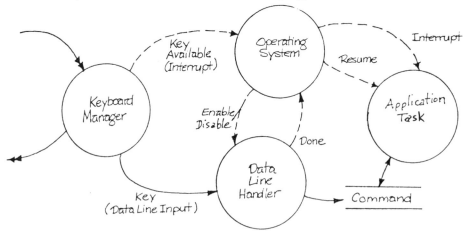

Figure 6.7 Complete SILLY keyboard interface.

It can be seen from the last example that an interface utility can be a dedicated processor like the keyboard manager, or a task within a processor like the data line handler. An interface utility could also be implemented as a subordinate routine called within an application task.

Although the ideal implementation environment is invisible to the application code, there are portions of interactive interfaces so application-specific that they may not be worth defining as general-purpose utilities. Let's once more turn to the example of SILLY. In the essential model, user commands simply "flow" to the appropriate transformation with no routing necessary. If the essential model transformations are implemented by separate tasks within a processor, and if the commands come from a single source (the Command store in Figure 6.7), some mechanism to distribute the commands to the appropriate tasks is necessary. Although a general purpose "command-to-task distributor" could be defined, it can be argued that the distribution mechanism is better incorporated within the implementation model, as illustrated in general terms by Figure 6.8.

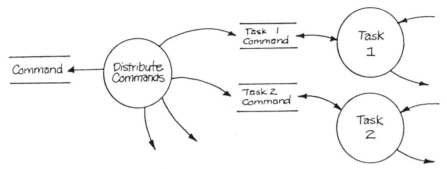

Figure 6.8 SILLY command distribution.

The second category of system utility is a *transformation utility.* Unlike interface utilities, transformation utilities actually do some of the work described by the essential model. Mathematical utilities, such as those for differential and integral equation solution, fall into this category.

Transformation utilities can be identified by *generalization* from the essential model. In other words, the modeler identifies part of an essential model transformation that is a special case of a more general transformation, and defines the work to be done at the more general semantic level. As an example, consider the transformation specification for Check Sheet Statuses from the Defect system (Appendix B of Volume 2). The logic describes checking for specific location values corresponding to the positions of the scanner, chopper, and other inspection surface components, and issuing a specific event flow when such a location is found. If the idea of data abstractions is applied, this can be seen as a special case of checking an input value V against an array of significant values $SV(I)$ where I ranges from 1 to N, and issuing a message $M(J)$ corresponding to the index J if $V = SV(J)$ for some J in the range of 1 to N. The essential model work could thus be implemented by defining such a table for the inspection surface and executing the appropriate utility routine (or possibly a single processor instruction).

Transformation utilities are commonly implemented as tasks or portions of tasks subordinated by a call relationship to the application code.

The third category of system utility is a *control utility.* Like transformation utilities, control utilities implement portions of the essential model. However, instead of transforming application data, control utilities implement the dynamic structure of the essential model. This is done by incorporating a portion of an essential model state transition diagram; a control utility may implement a state transition, or permit the operation of concurrent transformations.

The need for control utilities often arises when essential model transformations have been allocated to separate tasks within a single processor. For example, in the Bottling System (Appendix B in Volume 2), assume that the Control Input Valve and Control pH transformations have been assigned to separate tasks. Since these transformations must operate over the same time period, some element of the system above the level of the individual tasks must simulate the concurrency. The operation of the tasks could be managed by a general-purpose task dispatching utility, which uses a table of task IDs and required activation rates. Such a utility could also manage state transitions by maintaining a table of task statuses (active or passive) as a function of state. A given task would be activated at a particular time only if its status were active.

Like transformation utilities, control utilities are identified by generalization from the essential model. Operating systems, in fact, are very general control utilities that provide processing and memory resources to other pieces of software within a processor at appropriate times.

6.5 Cross references between application and utility models

We have advocated defining system utilities by building models that are separate from the implementation models of the primary system to be built. However, these separate models must have sufficient detail to permit integration of the application and the utilities when the system is built and run. The discussion in this section will focus mostly on references to system utilities from the application model, but can also be applied to the reverse situation.

Effective ways to reference a system utility from an implementation model parallel the actual connection between the implemented systems. Let's consider three types of connections — calls, communication areas, and configuration data — in terms of the binding time of the connection and of the type of data involved.

A *call* consists of the setup by the calling routine of a data structure (parameter list) to be made available to the called routine, plus the actual transfer and return of control. The call mechanism operates at run time, and the data transferred is usually subject-matter data as defined by the essential model. It is important to recognize that a call is the implementation of a flow or store connection and does not change the overall structure of a model (Figure 6.9).

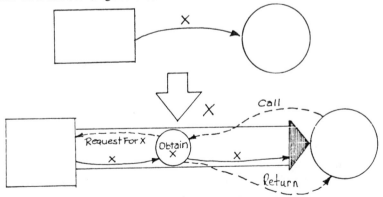

Figure 6.9 Call as implementation of a flow connection.

Therefore a call can be represented as an annotation on a data specification, or as an annotation on a transformation specification. Figure 6.10 shows a task within the SILLY implementation model.

Figure 6.10 SILLY implementation task.

The flow **Trigger Word Command** is a composite of the keyboard commands used in conjunction with a trigger word modification. If the keyboard input is to be obtained by a call, the data specification can be made accordingly:

Trigger Word Command = [0 | 1 | 2...F | Scroll Left | Scroll Right | Bin | Hex]
              * implement using the READKBD call — stored in library #XYZ *

If a specific type of call to obtain or send data is to be used by a number of tasks, the annotation can be made on the data specification of a high-level composite flow incorporating all of the lower-level flows:

User Command = [Logic Acquisition Command | Trigger Command |
                Display Manipulation Command]

                          implement using the READKBD call — stored in library #XYZ

The call just described activates an interface utility and implements a flow connection from the environment to the system. Calls to transformation utilities often implement an internal flow connection between fragments of a transformation. Therefore the use of the call can be documented as an annotation of the transformation specification. In the example of the Check Sheet Statuses transformation in Section 6.4 of this chapter, the comment:

    use calls to TABLEINIT, TABLECHECK as per library #ABC

could be added to the transformation specification.

A *communication area* is simply a segment of memory known to both an application task and a system utility and used to communicate data. A communication area is often defined at load time by means of an external variable declared within the application task, and is used to transfer application data. The use of a communication area is an implementation of a flow or store connection as is the call, and can be documented in the implementation model in the same way. For example, if keyboard commands in SILLY were to be implemented by a communication area, the appropriate data specification could be annotated with

    Define a one-byte external variable EXKBD.

The use of communication areas places more responsibility on the application code than does the use of calls. In the example just given, the task that receives keyboard input has no external protection against checking the communication area several times between changes made by the utility, and concluding that several identical commands have been issued. Please refer to the discussion in Section 5.3 of Chapter 5, Interface Modeling.

Configuration data refers to data about the structure of a model, or about the connections between models, rather than to subject-matter data transformed by a system. Configuration data often consists of a representation in data terms of the patterns of movement of data and control of an implementation model. For example, let's assume that conditions X, Y, and Z on the state transition diagram of Figure 6.11 are to be implemented as interrupts. If the activation and deactivation of tasks is to be handled by a table-driven task dispatcher (as modeled in Figure 6.12), the implementation model should contain a tabular form of the state transition diagram as a supplement to the graphic model, as shown in Table 6.1. The structure of the essential model is therefore represented *as data within* the utility.

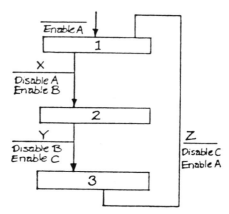

Figure 6.11 State diagram to be implemented with task dispatcher.

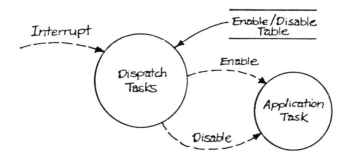

Figure 6.12 Task dispatcher model.

Interrupt	Tasks Enabled	Tasks Disabled
X	B	A
Y	C	B
Z	A	C
⋮	⋮	⋮

Table 6.1 Configuration data for task dispatcher.

Configuration data about the structure of the essential model can be made available to a system utility at compile time or at load time. However, data about connections between an application task and a utility can be dynamic, in which case it will have to be modifiable at run time. If system outputs are displayed on a screen by a graphics handler, for example, the user may need to change the graphic representation of a specific output as the system is operating. The transformations that handle the run-time modification of configuration data are at a semantic level "between" the semantic levels of the application and the utility. Such transformations may be incorporated into the implementation model of the application, or may be modeled separately as a configuration data utility.

6.6 System utilities in a multi-project environment

When a "family" of related systems is to be implemented by a systems development project, a set of well-designed utilities can significantly reduce the work required. The ideal is to build for each system in the family a minimal superstructure of application-specific code. Within this superstructure, pre-existing utilities may be assembled tinker-toy fashion to create a working system. The UNIX® system provides a set of utilities of this type together with a powerful mechanism for creating a superstructure.

6.7 Summary

An effective implementation strategy requires careful separation of subject-matter-specific details from details that can be handled by general systems support utilities. To attain this end, it is important to be able to visualize a support utility as a system in its own right, divorced from the semantics of the application it will support. This chapter has presented guidelines for identifying required support functions and for building models of system utilities.

Chapter 6: References

1. Information Processing Systems — Open Systems Interconnection — Basic Reference Model. Draft International Standard ISO/DIS 7498, 1982.

2. K.H. Britton, R.A. Parker, and D.L. Parnas. *A Procedure for Designing Abstract Interfaces for Device Interface Models.* Proceedings, Fifth International Conference on Software Engineering, IEE, 1981, pp. 195-204.

7
Modeling System Services
— Data Management

7.1 Introduction

Nearly all essential models require event responses to communicate with one another via stored data. The corresponding implementation models thus must include a description of the stored data implementation. The stored data that must be available to the tasks within a single processor is shown by the portion of the entity-relationship diagram (or the equivalent set of transformation schema stores) allocated to that processor and by the associated data specifications. Data that is shared among a set of processors is thought of as belonging to each of the processors. In this chapter, we shall focus on modeling the implementation of and access to stored data shared among tasks within a processor. We shall also discuss modeling the co-ordination required when stored data is duplicated among processors.

7.2 Stored data management technology

Widespread and uncontrolled sharing of data between tasks is generally, and quite correctly, regarded as poor design practice because it violates the general criterion of organizing for maximum implementation independence. Nevertheless, data must be shared to the extent required by the essential model; the problem is to reduce the dangers implicit in this sharing to a minimum.

This problem has been faced before in commercial systems, and it has led to the development of a specialized technology — database management systems, databases, inquiry languages and the like. However the volume of data in such systems is often larger than in typical real-time systems and the access time requirements are often not as stringent. Data management technology has therefore become associated with the use of disk storage and with (relatively) slow access times, and consequently many reject the use of the technology in real-time systems. We feel that this is an error for several reasons. First, many real-time systems do in fact store relatively large quantities of data that can be accessed within the time constraints of disk technology. Second, the concepts of data management technology do not limit themselves to disk storage implementations. Third, these ideas, even if they can only be applied as restricted by real-time timing constraints, still provide significant benefits as guidelines to stored data organization.

Let us begin by defining some terms. A *database* is a collection of shared stored data items. It is important to distinguish the data that makes up the database from any software that manipulates the data, and from the organization or description of the data. A shared common block between several FORTRAN programs matches our definition of a database. A *data description language* is a (usually textual) means for describing the organization of the data that exists or will exist in a database. The term *data schema* is often used for the resulting description; however, we have reserved this term for the entity-relationship diagram and its supporting specifics. We draw a distinction between our use of the terms *data schema* and *data description* by restricting the latter term to a description of the data that is processed by some specific collection of database software. (To the best of our knowledge there is no currently available software that can use the data schema as we use the term to define the organization of a physical database). *Data access methods* are mechanisms that use the data description of a database to access data in a database. These terms are defined in more detail in [1].

This restricted set of definitions is sufficient to enable us to demonstrate the useful data management concepts. In a real-time system stored data exists and is shared (a database); the static organization of data and its use by tasks is defined (data description languages); and data is referred to and manipulated through knowledge of its organization (via data access methods). Typically, the data description language and data access methods are implemented via a programming language. In FORTRAN, for example, data is defined via common block definitions and accessed by name from the programming language.

The next two sections examine design criteria that motivate the development and use of data management technology.

7.3 Data independence and binding

Consider a commonly found implementation of stored data: there is a single globally accessible shared data area, whose organization is defined by the data definition facilities of the chosen programming language; every task in the system that shares data is compiled with the definition of the entire shared area, and thus has access to all the data at any time. There are several problems in this scheme. First, no protection is provided for any of the data elements; if a data element exhibits an incorrect value, there are no clues as to which task modified the element since all tasks have access. Second, any change in the structure of the stored data will lead to recompilation of all tasks in the system. Since all tasks assume the same structure for the data, then if any one task changes its view, all tasks must follow suit. Typically, this is time-consuming and error-prone, which leads many programmers into taking short cuts, such as finding an unallocated area of memory and making private agreements on the use of this area between the tasks that share it. Third, data access mechanisms are specific to each task, which leads to duplication of effort and further dependence on the present data structure. Clearly, this scheme has significant disadvantages; however, it is fast. References to data locations can be resolved at compilation time so that data elements can be accessed simply by a reference to an address.

In its attempt to overcome these problems, a key objective of data management technology is the achievement of *data independence;* that is, each task should be unaware of the storage structure and access mechanism of the data accessed. If data independence is achieved, stored data can be reorganized with no impact on the code of each task. Data management technology achieves data independence by interposing one or more layers of system software between the application task and access to the data itself. In this way, a call is made to a system software task which then *uses a data description* to access the data item. These "additional" layers of code may introduce inefficiencies into the implementation, which can cause problems in a real-time system.

The efficiency and independence objectives are clearly in conflict. The two objectives can be studied together by introducing the concept of *binding* [2]. In compiler theory, a name is said to be *bound* to a location when the location is associated with the name. (The term is also used to refer to the association of a name to an identifier, and the association of a value to a name.) In the case of a single globally shared data area whose definition is compiled into each process, the names are bound to locations at compile time (or if the location of the shared area is not fixed, at link/load time). On the other hand, the use of a procedure to access a data item will delay the binding until run time. It is the execution of the binding at run-time that causes the use of data management technology to be less efficient, yet more independent.

Table 7.1 summarizes the independence and efficiency characteristics of different binding times.

Binding Time	Impact Of Changing Data Definition	Impact On Run-Time Efficiency	Data Location Associated With
Run-Time	None	Slows-Down Processing	Task-Independent Data Description
Initialize Time	Restart Task	Slows Down Initialization	Task Independent Data Description
Load/Link Time	Relink/ Reload Task	None	Data Structures In Loaded Program
Compile Time	Recompile Task	None	Data Structures In Compiled Program
Code Time	Re-Code Task	None	Processing Instructions In Compiled Program

(Increasing Data Independence — top; Increasing Efficiency — bottom)

Table 7.1 Characteristics of various strategies for stored data access.

7.4 Organization of data

There are two faces to data organization implementation: the view that is presented to the designer and programmer, and the actual physical organization of the data on the chosen storage media. The designer and the programmer will want to perform operations on data structures according to an *external* view of how the data is grouped and organized; this can be separated from the *internal* data structure chosen for the data. It is the business of any data management software to provide mechanisms to manipulate the external data structure which can then be translated into operations on the internal data structure.

There are three basic approaches to organizing data structures [3] each of which applies to both the external and internal models. Often, it is natural to use the same approach for both models; though it is by no means necessary. These approaches are:

- the relational approach, in which the basic data structure is a table, or

- the hierarchical approach, in which data is stored in hierarchical trees and there is only one path to a given data category, or

- the network (or CODASYL) approach, in which data is stored in a network of nodes and there may be several paths to a given data category.

The approach chosen will affect the operations that can be carried out on the data structures. The remainder of this section describes the three *external* views of data. The internal structure chosen may match exactly, or may be chosen to be different for efficiency reasons.

Consider the entity-relationship diagram shown in Figure 7.1, which is derived from the Defect Inspection System (Appendix D). The relational approach would view the data organization as a set of tables, as shown in Figure 7.2.

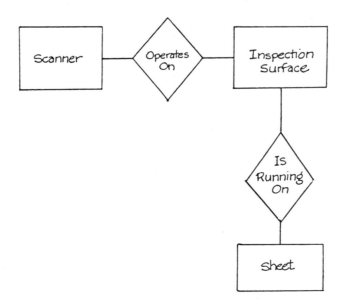

Figure 7.1 Entity-relationship diagram to be represented in data.

In this case, the relationships are implemented by data elements that refer to other tables. (For example, to find out which inspection surface sheet 105 is running on, we examine an additional data element for the sheet that specifies the identifier of the inspection surface.)

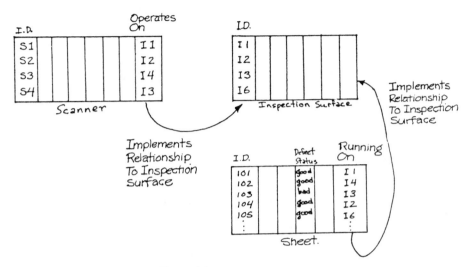

Figure 7.2 Data in relational tables.

Contrast this organization to a hierarchical storage model as shown in Figure 7.3. In this case, the relationships are implemented by *pointers* rather than as data. If the system were to need to mark all sheets scanned by a scanner as BAD in response to a fault in the scanner, it is necessary to move *up* the tree to find the associated inspection surface, then *down* the tree to find all the sheets running on that surface.

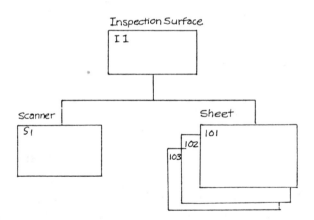

Figure 7.3 Hierarchal representation.

The network approach, however, could obviate the need for this step by choosing to have two parents (or owners) for the sheets as shown in Figure 7.4. This design might be necessary if scanners failed frequently and the time taken to navigate the structure was too long.

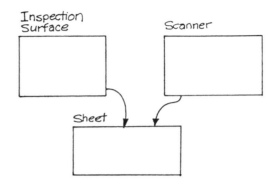

Figure 7.4 Network representation.

Once an approach is chosen, and the appropriate manipulation procedures are either written or purchased, the total volume of code can be significantly reduced. Returning for a moment to Figure 7.2 (the relational model), if the task is to set all occurrences of a sheet that has been misscanned by a failed scanner, then the code is simply:

Find the inspection surface for the failed scanner
Find all the sheets that are running on that inspection surface
Set the defect status for all these sheets to BAD

Please note that *find* and *set* are simply general queries on the data that can be implemented just once and used in many contexts. We shall detail similar operations in subsequent sections.

7.5 Advantages of an external relational view

A unified external view of data has several advantages. First, designers and programmers need have only a single standardized set of data manipulation operations and data structures to understand, rather than several idiosyncratic ones. Second, data can be reorganized without affecting code as a result of data independence. Third, data may be reallocated between primary and secondary memory transparently [4].

We shall discuss in this section a relational organization of data. We have chosen this approach for the external view of data for the following reasons. First, the underlying data structure is extremely simple (tables). This allows the designer to construct procedures that assume a single, simple data structure. Second, connections among operations on data are independent of the implementation. For example, consider two tasks, one which finds which inspection surface a scanner is running, and another which sets the defect statuses for all the sheets on an inspection surface, as shown in Figure 7.5. In a relational model, the data flow between the two is the identifier of the inspection surface. In a hierarchical model such as the one in Figure 7.3, the result of the equivalent task that finds the inspection surface would have as output a *pointer* to the inspection surface. The task that changes the defect status would have to be designed to accept the pointer; this would then make the task useless if the pointer mechanism were to be modified. Similar problems appear if a network approach is utilized. Third, embedded real-time systems tend to have complex environments which are liable to be expanded, modified, or reconfigured [5]. This places a burden on the designer to construct a system that can withstand frequent modifications to the data structures and the code that operates on them. Since the relational approach represents connections between tables *in data*, the connections are bound at run-time — a more general approach than the alternatives.

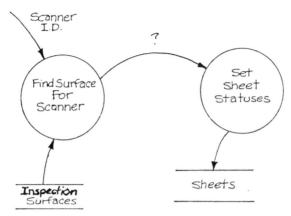

Figure 7.5 A data identifier as an intermediate flow.

Relational databases have a reputation for being slow, even in a commercial system environment. The generality of the approach and the late binding of data to implement relationships tend to justify this reputation. However, as we stated earlier, it is not necessary to use the same storage approach internally. For example, a relational interface could be constructed that, for certain queries, operates on data in memory stored as relational tables, but translates other queries to a network database on disk. This scheme would then present a common unified view of data to designers and programmers that is independent of the internal organization. Data may be allocated to memory or to a disk based on, first, speed of access, and, second, complexity of required queries. (The complexity of a query will have an impact on speed.) The allocation strategy is summarized in Table 7.2.

Speed Of Query \ Complexity Of Query	Simple	Complex
Slow	Independent Files On Disk	Files On Disk
Fast	Primary Storage	

Table 7.2 Storage choices by query type.

In the next section, we address the external operations that manipulate stored data in the relational approach.

7.6 Run-time database manipulation operations

Stored data is manipulated by tasks: data is retrieved, computations are carried out, and data is stored. To preserve data independence, the retrieval and storage activities should be independent of the precise data items that are being accessed. Again, data management technology can provide us with some guidelines.

The two basic operations we require are SELECT, which chooses a set of rows from a table according to some criteria, and PROJECT, which chooses a set of columns from a table. For this discussion, we'll assume that the results of the operations are table descriptors; data can then be accessed by GET and PUT operations. Referring to Figures 7.1 and 7.2, the code to flag all sheets checked by a faulty scanner as BAD is:

```
* find the scanner
scanner-table ← OPEN (SCANNER)
broken-scanner-table ← SELECT (scanner-table, SCANNER-ID=input-scanner-id)

* find which inspection surface it's on
operating-on ← PROJECT (broken-scanner-table, OPERATES-ON)
inspection-surface ← GET (operating-on)

* find the sheets in the inspection surface
sheet-table ← OPEN (SHEET)
bad-sheet-table ← SELECT (sheet-table, RUNNING-ON = inspection-surface)

* identify the defect status column
defect-table ← PROJECT (bad-sheet-table, DEFECT-STATUS)

* set the defect status
PUT (defect-table, "bad")
```

The upper case variable names are strings that are searched for at run-time in a data description; this allows for the data that represents each data element to be stored anywhere. The table descriptions simply identify the elements being accessed, and the shared data is passed to or from the task only by GET and PUT operations.

Many simplifying assumptions have been made: adds and deletes are not allowed during the operation of the task, operations are defined only for single tables, elimination of duplicate rows is not carried out, and we have not defined the organization of the workspace in the task. Nevertheless, we have achieved many of the advantages described in the previous sections.

A third relational operation, the JOIN, may also be made available. The join operation constructs a new table from rows in the input tables by matching from columns that have a common domain. The resulting table typically contains redundancy. In the general case, the join operation is a time-consuming process, and is therefore often inappropriate in a run-time system. However, if the resulting table is operated on frequently, it may be advantageous to perform the join offline and store the resulting table in primary storage. In this case, all tasks that operate on the table are less independent of the data structure than is desirable because they must account for the redundancy.

7.7 Constructing relational tables in primary memory

The data schema for each processor provides a basis for an allocation between primary and secondary memory. Each data element should be tagged appropriately as indicated by Table 7.2. We now focus only on elements allocated to primary memory.

Each object type becomes a table in which each data element is a column of the table, and each occurrence is a row. The physical representation of each data element should be defined, and the actual (or maximum) number of occurrences in the table should also be specified. This information constitutes a *data description.*

Relationships are also represented as tables. When the relationship between object-types is one-to-many, an additional column may be added to the object-type on the "many" side of the relationship that contains data that identifies a unique occurrence of the other object-type. When the relationship is one-to-one, the additional column may be added to either object-type. When the relationship is many-to-many, a new table should be constructed which contains references to unique occurrences of each participating object-type. The columns of the resulting table should contain elements that make up the identifiers of the appropriate object-types. Again, the characteristics of the columns and tables should be added to the data description.

The data description produced by the translation of the entity-relationship diagram into relational tables may serve as input to a preprocessor (a data description language translator) that allocates space in primary memory and builds tables that describe the allocation. These tables are then used by the data manipulation operations to find and access run-time data. [6]

In the next section, we shall describe how the data description may be used to speed access to stored data.

7.8 Speeding access to stored data

From the data description, the data description translator produces an allocation for the tables defined for the application. This allocation may contain absolute addresses or addresses relative to the base of the shared data area. The data manipulation operations described in Section 7.6 bind names within a task to these locations at run-time. In certain situations, this may be too slow to meet implementation constraints.

GET and PUT operations in time-critical tasks may be translated into direct accesses to memory by a preprocessor applied to code written in the language of choice, since the addresses referred to by name are known by the data description translator. This technique binds names to locations at preprocessing/compilation time, and will require recompilation of all such tasks if the data description changes. It also requires that tables may not be added or deleted. Nevertheless, many of the advantages of data independence are still accrued.

This technique can be carried further. If static data is operated on by SELECT and PROJECT operations, these operations may be *executed on a copy of the static data at preprocessing time.* The processing load is transferred away from run-time into the non-time-critical construction activities.

A less radical approach may be taken that still has the advantage of shifting processing load away from run-time computations. Resolution of names into addresses may be carried out by initialization tasks that compute pointers to the data to be operated on, and pass these pointers to run-time tasks.

7.9 Distributed databases

In a multiprocessor environment, the stored data derived from the essential entity-relationship diagram will be fragmented across several processors, and some of the data will be duplicated as described in Chapter 3, Processor Modeling. The physical data schemas for each processor are annotated with references to the master version of each data element from which others are duplicated. However, the activity of duplicating the data elements has not yet been modeled. The issue at hand, therefore, is to decide when each data element must be copied from the application's point of view. Please note that tasks to carry out the copying qualify as system software and can therefore be modeled using the techniques of system software modeling as described in Chapter 6.

Data items representing continuous variables that are updated by periodic tasks are candidates for periodic copying between processors. The interval chosen for the copying is dependent on the use the *receiver* makes of the data. For example, a task may monitor and control a particular device at very short intervals; an operator may also be interested in examining the data being used for the monitoring. It is most unlikely that an operator will wish to see this updated data as frequently as it changes, and a much more leisurely pace may be appropriate. It is therefore the receiver that determines the rate of any periodic update between processors.

Discrete data elements may also be copied periodically between processors. Each cycle, all the chosen data elements are copied regardless of whether they have been changed. This is a simple way of keeping data consistent between processors, so long as the data items are not internally inconsistent across any cycle. Discrete data elements may also be copied between processors only when the data element is *changed.* This may be implemented by the interposition of database management software between tasks that change data and the actual database so that changed data elements can be marked as needing to be copied, or by explicitly making a request to copy certain data elements. The task that carries out the copy may keep data that describes the destination task(s) of groups of data elements.

Variations and combinations of these techniques are also possible. For example, whole blocks of data might be marked to be copied even if only one element in the block has changed. Similarly, all discrete changes of data elements may be collected and transmitted periodically. The choice between these various techniques should be made on the basis of data consistency, permitted delays in modifying updated data in the destination processor, and the capacity of the transmission links as described in Section 5.3 of Chapter 5, Interface Modeling.

7.10 Summary

The techniques of data management technology are applicable in real-time systems. However, the costs, particularly the run-time efficiency costs and the benefits, must be carefully weighed. The later the binding time, the more likely the system is to be data independent and easy to modify, but it is likely to be less efficient.

Chapter 7: References

1. C.J. Date, *An Introduction to Data Base Systems* (second edition), Reading: Addison Wesley, 1977.

2. A.V. Aho and J.D. Ullman, *Principles of Compiler Design*, Reading: Addison Wesley, 1977.

3. Op. cit. [1].

4. I.M. Willers and D.N. Wilner, *Overview of the ICS Database*, Lawrence Berkeley Laboratory and Bay Area Rapid Transit District, 1981.

5. Sally Shlaer and Stephen J. Mellor, *Modeling the World in Data*, New York: Yourdon Press, to be published in 1986. 1981.

6. Op. cit. [5].

Section 3

Module Stage Tools
and Heuristics

The three chapters of this section explore the final stage of the implementation model, which is concerned with the organization of units of code within a task.

Chapter 8, Modeling Hierarchy, introduces a notation specifically designed to illuminate module-level organization, that of the structure chart.

Chapter 9, Translating Networks into Hierarchies, provides procedures for allocating portions of the task-level implementation model to modules and module connections.

Chapter 10, Structure Chart Refinement, discusses the application of quality criteria to the module-level model.

8
Modeling Hierarchy

8.1 Introduction

The modeling guidelines set forth in Chapters 3 and 4 (Processor Modeling and Task Modeling) of this volume describe the creation of a hierarchy of transformation schemas. The top level of this hierarchy has one transformation for each processor into which part of the essential model has been allocated. The next lower level consists of a schema for each processor, with transformations representing the tasks into which that processor's portion of the essential model has been allocated. The lowest level of the hierarchy has a schema for each task. These schemas contain portions of the essential model that have been modified to remove concurrency and continuous processing and to centralize control. The modifications remove any barriers to translating the lowest-level schemas into sequential code; although the transformation schema is inherently capable of representing non-sequential processing, these particular schemas represent purely sequential processing.

In certain cases, the translation into code is direct and obvious. For example, the pair of transformations that sample and control continuous inputs whose control logic is represented in Figure 4.13 can be translated directly into linear code, or into a controlling routine with its called subroutines. However, a more complicated low-level schema may not have such an obvious realization as code.

There is a large family of commonly used programming languages, excluding APL and LISP but including FORTRAN, Pascal, Ada®, and many assembler languages, that permit a hierarchical structure mediated by the subroutine call mechanism. For tasks to be coded in one of these languages, a model that allows visualization and refinement of a subroutine hierarchy can be extremely useful. This chapter will describe such a model. The schematic portion of this model is the *structure chart,* and the specifics are modeled using *module specifications* and *data specifications.*

8.2 The structure chart

The basic units of the structure chart are the *module,* the *call,* the *shared data area* and the *couple.* The first two are concerned with the active processing units of the task, and the last two focus on the data used by the active units. Each will be described in turn. Much more detailed presentations of the structure chart may be found in [1,2]. These presentations place less emphasis on the shared data area than does the treatment in this chapter and the following chapters.

The module is a single, named, independently callable unit of code managed by the control structure of a task. This definition is similar in many ways to the definition of a task; however, only one module may be active at a time in a task, whereas several tasks may be active concurrently. Different programming languages have different implementations of the module and give them different names: procedure, typed procedure, function, subroutine, and the like. The module is modeled as a box with the name of the module placed in the box, as shown in Figure 8.1.

Figure 8.1 A module.

The call is an activation of a module. When a calling module executes a call to a subordinate, the calling module is no longer active. When the subordinate completes its job, control is returned to the caller at the point in the caller's logic immediately after the call. Please note that the call differs from the enable/disable of the transformation schema in that the calling module becomes inactive when the call is issued and remains inactive until the called module returns control when it has completed its job, whereas the producer of an enable remains active and may disable the called module at any time. The call is modeled by an arrow pointing from the caller to the called module as shown in Figure 8.2. A call is modeled if there is *any* occurrence of a call in the caller irrespective of the number of calls that will be executed at run time.

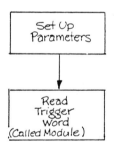

Figure 8.2 A module call.

The shared data area represents data that is shared among several modules. The data is accessible to all modules that share the area and survives between calls to any of the participating modules. A shared data area and its modules are similar to a *package* in Ada; the grouping is sometimes called an "information cluster." The shared data area is modeled as a box drawn below each module that shares the data. The name of the area is written within the box. An example of modules sharing static data is shown in Figure 8.3. Drawing modules that share a data area as adjacent, as done in Figure 8.3, emphasizes their close connection, but is not required. A shared data area used by only a single module represents "state memory" that survives between calls.

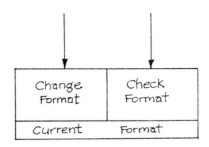

Figure 8.3 Shared data area.

The couple represents an item of data (a parameter) passed between modules when a call is executed. Data may be passed from the caller to the called module or vice versa. Couples are modeled as small arrows (placed near the appropriate call) that point in the direction that the data flows (Figure 8.4). At the other end of the arrow a small circle is drawn. An open circle represents data that is processed. A filled-in circle represents control information that controls the logic of the receiver. All couples must be named, and the name is the name used by the *caller*. This results in more specific data names; low-level modules often perform utility functions and have a semantic level that is remote from that of the application.

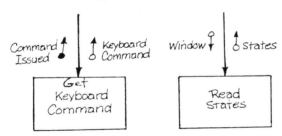

Figure 8.4 Couples.

To create a complete structure chart, the notational elements are combined into a tree structure as illustrated in Figure 8.5. Note that a module may be called by more than one parent. However, the model represents a true hierarchy since an active lower-level module is always "owned" by only one of the possible parents.

In summary, the structure chart is used for modeling the partitioning of a task into modules, the hierarchical organization of these modules, and both the active and passive data interfaces between them.

As with all our models, the schematic view provided by the structure chart is not adequate unless it is supported by specifics for each of the pieces. In the next two sections, we describe tools for specifying the processing (module specifications) and the data (data specifications).

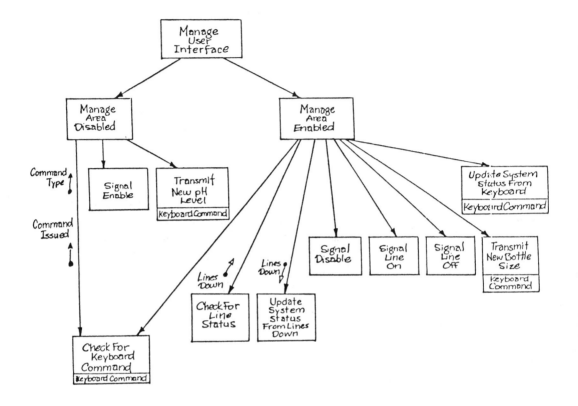

Figure 8.5 A structure chart.

8.3 The module specification

Each module declared on the structure chart must be accompanied by a module specification. The goal is for each module to be defined so that it can be coded correctly, yet we do not wish to carry out the actual programming at this stage.

Many of the modules will be derived directly from fragments of the essential model as allocated to units of the implementation. The same tools used for describing these essential model fragments may continue to be used — pre/post conditions, structured language, pseudocode, and the like. Please refer to Chapter 8 of Volume 1, Specifying Transformations, for a discussion of these tools. The amount of detail provided in the specification should depend on the destination language: there is little use in writing detailed pseudocode for a module to be written in a high-level language such as Ada, whereas if the destination language is a low-level language such as microcode, it may be much more appropriate.

8.4 The data specification

Both couples and shared data areas must be specified. As with the module specification, many of the data specifications required can be drawn directly from the allocated essential model. There are, however, some implementation details not addressed during essential modeling that must be accounted for.

First, the *representation* of each data element must be defined; the essential model merely defines range and precision or the domain of a data element. We must now choose an appropriate representation for the element: integer, real, bit pattern, and the like, as well as any limits imposed on values that can be taken on. Higher-level languages such as Ada take away the need to define some of these details. In lower-level languages, the representation and limits should be added as comments to the data element definition.

Second, the *ordering* of data elements in a structure may be defined. Again, higher-level languages often allow a structure's components to be accessed by name, and therefore the ordering is irrelevant. Lower-level languages may require the definition of displacements from the base pointer of a data structure. The amount of space that must be allocated for each item is specified by the chosen representation; if the order of elements is important, the data structure should be tagged as such in the data dictionary by a comment.

Third, shared data areas may require specification of *initial values* to be set when the system is loaded or at initialization time. If Ada is used, this data specification will become the basis for the initialization section for the package. On the other hand, if lower level languages are used, the specification may be used as the basis of DATA statements in FORTRAN, or as a module to be called when the process is activated.

8.5 Summary

The structure chart and its associated specifics constitute a model of the module organization of a task. The structure chart specifically accounts for the sequential and hierarchical nature of many of today's programming languages, thus bridging the gap between the transformation schema and the code.

Chapter 8: References

1. Ed Yourdon and L. Constantine, *Structured Design*, New York: Yourdon Press, 1978.

2. Meilir Page-Jones, *The Practical Guide to Structured Systems Design*, New York: Yourdon Press, 1980.

9

Translating Networks into Hierarchies

9.1 Introduction

The translation of the transformation schema into a structure chart is a translation of a network representation of the activities of a task into a hierarchical representation; the result serves as a basis for writing the code. The translation should introduce as little distortion as possible. To guarantee this, first the translation must retain the separation of the management or controlling work of the process from the data transformation work. In the transformation schema, this division is represented by the separation of control transformations from data transformations. Second, we wish to keep separate the essential model work from necessary implementation work such as formatting data structures for input and output. Third, since the transformation schema does not explicitly represent the work of moving data, we wish to keep the portions of the hierarchy that move data separate from the portions that transform data, making the data transformation portions independent of the specifics of the hierarchy and thus reusable. Fourth, we wish to separate data that passes across a common interface into its use by different essential model fragments as rapidly as possible, so that if the structure of the data for one essential model fragment should change then the processing is not inextricably tangled with the processing for other fragments.

In this chapter, we describe techniques for accomplishing this translation with minimum distortion.

9.2 Finding the top of the hierarchy

The top of the hierarchy in a structure chart is responsible for the controlling decisions of the activity of the task. This is the same role played by the control transformation on the transformation schema; therefore, the basic structure of the control transformation will translate into the upper-level module structure. The data transformations connected to the control transformation will become lower-level modules.

If no control transformation has been allocated to the task, then a controlling module must be invented to manage all of the data transformations. The manager module may then call each of the subordinates, honoring any sequencing specified by the transformation schema. If data produced by a data transformation is required by another data transformation, then the predecessor transformation must produce its data first. On the other hand, if each data transformation is independent, they may be executed in an arbitrary sequence.

9.3 Translating transformation schemas with control transformations

If the modeling techniques decribed in Section 4.3 of Chapter 4, Task Modeling, have been applied, each transformation schema will have at most a single control transformation.

It is possible to encode the logic of a control transformation in an ad-hoc manner by constructing code for each transition and using labels to distinguish states. However, the non-sequential nature of the state diagram does not readily match the sequential nature of code, leading to unstructured code which fails to take advantage of the regular structure of the specification. The following code illustrates some of the problems for the state transition diagram shown in Figure 9.1 (from the Cruise Control mechanism described in Appendix A).

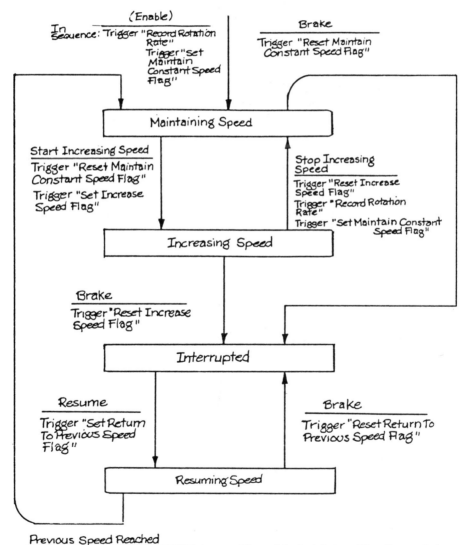

Figure 9.1 A state transition diagram to be encoded.

module Control Mode of Operation
      record rotation rate
      set maintain constant speed flag
   maintaining speed:
      get condition (: condition)
      if condition = start increasing speed **then**
        reset Maintain Constant Speed flag
        set Increase Speed flag
      else
        if condition = brake **then**
          reset Maintain Constant Speed flag
          go to Interrupted
        else
          error ("illegal condition", condition:)
          go to maintaining speed
        endif
      endif
   increasing speed:
      get condition (: condition)
      if condition = stop increasing speed **then**
        Reset Increase Speed flags
        record rotation rate
        set Maintain Constant Speed flag
        go to maintaining speed
      else
        if condition = brake **then**
          reset increase speed flag
        else
          error ("illegal condition", condition:)
          go to increasing speed
        endif
      endif
   interrupted:
      get condition (: condition)
      if condition = resume **then**
        set Return to Previous Speed flag
      else
        error ("illegal condition", condition :)
        go to interrupted
      endif
   resuming speed:
      get condition (: condition)
      if condition = brake **then**
        reset Return to Previous Speed flag
        go to interrupted
      else
        if condition = previous speed reached **then**
          set Maintain Constant Speed flag
          reset Return to Previous Speed flag

```
            go to maintaining speed
        else
            error ("illegal condition", condition:)
            go to resuming speed
        endif
    endif
endmodule
```

The code above makes extensive use of "goto" statements and is therefore likely to be difficult to maintain. Furthermore, the only traces of the state diagram structure are the labels, which have no "enforcement" properties; statements can be inserted at will before or after a label.

In contrast to the code above, there are two more systematic approaches to representing a control transformation on a structure chart: Either the entire transformation (that is, the associated state-transition diagram that specifies it) may be allocated to a single module, or the control transformation may be allocated to several modules — one module per state with a controlling module to select among the submodules. The first strategy requires casting the specification in terms of state transition and action tables as described in Volume 1, Chapter 7, Specifying Control Transformations and shown in Figure 9.2. In Figure 9.2, the actions have been replaced by module names that are called by the controlling module. The code for each of the submodules is simply the actions that were replaced.

	Maintaining Speed	Increasing Speed	Interrupted	Resuming Speed
start increasing speed	increasing speed / increase speed	increasing speed / error	interrupted / error	resuming speed / error
stop increasing speed	maintaining speed / error	maintaining speed / maintain speed	interrupted / error	resuming speed / error
brake	interrupted / interrupt maintenance	interrupted / interrupt speed increase	interrupted / error	interrupted / interrupt resumption
resume	maintaining speed / error	increasing speed / error	resuming speed / resume speed	resuming speed / error
previous speed reached	maintaining speed / error	increasing speed / error	interrupted / error	maintaining speed / resume maintenance

Figure 9.2 State transition and action table for Figure 9.1.

The code for the controlling module may now be written as follows:

module Traverse State Tables
        module ← initial module
        state ← initial state
        do forever
            do action (module:)
            get condition (:condition)
            module←Action Table (condition, state)
            state ← Transition Table (condition, state)
        endforever
    end module

Both Action Table and Transition Table are data structures that contain the names of the modules to be called as actions and the new states, respectively. The module Do Action takes the name of a module and calls it. The variables Initial Module and Initial State are used to make the transition into the initial state.

Do Action may be written in a variety of ways, depending on the programming language used. In a high-level language, the module names can be represented by constants that act as switches for explicit calls to modules. A new Do Action module must be written for each new table, since the *names* of the modules are written as code. In lower-level languages, the action table may be filled with the *addresses* of the module to be called. The module Do Action may then execute a module call on the address pointed to by the table.

The second strategy for translating a control transformation is to distribute control into several manager modules. This strategy leads to a controlling module that chooses which submodule to call, and one submodule for each state. Each submodule manages all possible transitions from the state, and returns the new state to its caller. A structure chart for the control transformation specification of Figure 9.1 is shown in Figure 9.3.

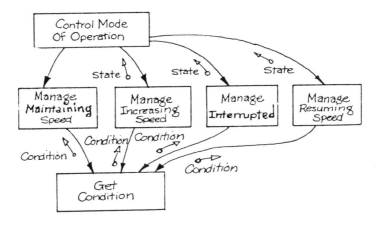

Figure 9.3 Top level structure chart for Figure 9.1.

The code for each of the submodules is to check for conditions that cause a transition, execute the appropriate actions, and return the new state. For example:

```
module  Manage Increase Speed
            get condition (: condition)
            if condition = brake then
               reset Increase Speed flag
               state ← interrupted
            else
               if condition = stop increasing speed then
                  reset increase speed flag
                  record rotation rate
                  set maintain constant speed flag
                  state ← maintaining speed
               else
                  error ("illegal condition", condition)
                  state ← increasing speed
               endif
            endif
endmodule
```

Note that waiting for the condition is placed in the submodule, rather than the controlling module. If a "snapshot" of the task is taken during a test while the task is waiting for a condition, it is possible to know which state the code is in by comparing the address of the suspended task with a load map since, for each state, the task will be waiting for a condition at a different location.

9.4 Module-level transformation schemas

The creation of structure charts from transformation schemas as described in the preceding sections is organized around the logic of a control transformation within the schema. However, it is often necessary to construct all or part of a structure chart from a transformation schema without benefit of a control transformation.

Consider a data transformation that accepts a transaction (that is, a set of data element values) from an operator and uses the information to update stored data; the transformation that changes the equipment configuration for the Defect Inspection System (Appendix D) is of this type. Such a transformation has no inherent control structure; it simply manipulates data and creates outputs when inputs are provided. However, the logic of the transformation may be complex enough to require an implementation with a hierarchy of modules and thus a control structure. This type of transformation may be implemented as a self-contained task, in which case an entire structure chart must be created to represent it. Or it may be within a task controlled by a control transformation, in which case the translation procedure will leave it as a single low-level module to be elaborated into a subhierarchy. The allocation of several isolated transformations to a single task also requires the construction of a hierarchy to control the allocated fragments. In all the above cases, a hierarchy must be built solely from one or more data transformations with no inherent control information.

Valuable information for determining the control structure of a structure chart may be gained by decomposing one or more data transformations into a *module-level transformation schema*. The decomposition process is guided by examining the internal data structure of the original data transformations. This examination can often identify sequential or parallel subtransformations based on required data manipulations. Consider a variation on the Bottle-Filling System transformation (Appendix B in Volume 2) that displays current pH to the area supervisor; assume that the transformation must average two readings from sensors with different characteristics as shown in Figure 9.4. This transformation may receive the sensor readings as arbitrary numeric values, convert them to engineering units, apply reasonableness checks, and convert the average into display format in addition to doing the averaging. The resultant module-level transformation schema is shown in Figure 9.5.

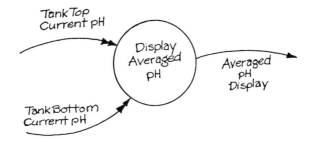

Figure 9.4 Data transformation in essential form.

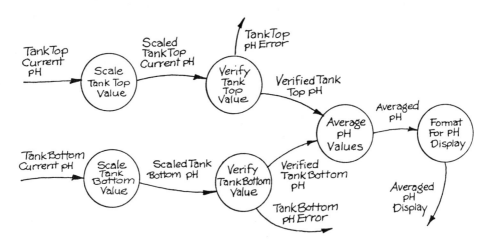

Figure 9.5 Module-level transformation schema.

The general categories of intermediate data that may assist in finding subtransformations are:

- input data as presented to the task by the environment

- input data in essential form

- input data in essential form suitable for normal processing

- output data in essential form

- output data in the form required for export to the environment.

(The decomposition process may aid in the detection of transformation utilities — Figure 9.5 could lead to a general-purpose scaling routine; see the discussion in Section 6.4 of Chapter 6.)

The transformation schema of Figure 9.5 has two parallel streams of transformations because of the separability of the inputs. It is also possible to identify parallelism based on separability of data elements or groups within a single input. Figure 9.6 shows the separation of the components of a transaction that requires verification of identifying data elements against two different data stores.

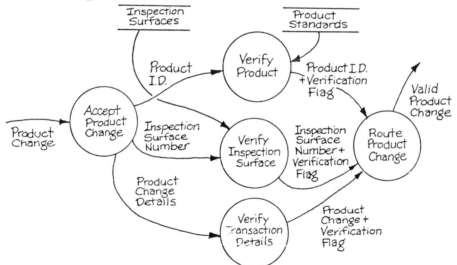

Figure 9.6 Parallel transformations on flow components.

9.5 Transform analysis

The module-level transformation schema of Figure 9.5 is the implementation of a single essential model transformation. This type of schema can be translated into a structure chart by a procedure known as *transform analysis* [1]. The procedure requires identification of the *central transform* of the schema, which corresponds to the transformation of input in its most essential form into output in its most essential form. There is no exact criterion for identifying a central transform; in practice excluding transformations that validate input, as well as transformations that change data from implementation to essential form or vice versa, leaves one or more transformations that are good candidates for a central transform. The Average pH Values transformation in Figure 9.5 is a reasonable choice. The transformations not belonging to the central transform

form one or more streams that are classified as *afferent* (bearing data to the central transform) and *efferent* (bearing data away from the central transform). Figure 9.7 shows the schema from Figure 9.5 annotated to show the various regions of the classification.

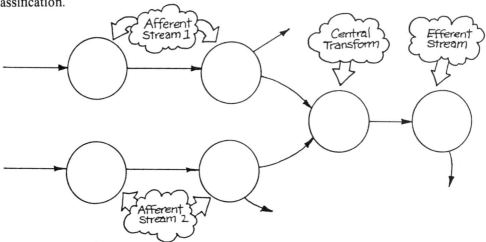

Figure 9.7 Transformation schema prepared for transform analysis.

The first stage in the translation consists of creating an upper-level structure chart framework with a controlling module, a second-level module for the central transform, and a second-level module for each afferent and efferent stream (Figure 9.8). All data to and from the afferent and efferent streams is routed through the central transform.

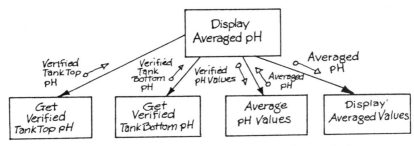

Figure 9.8 Preliminary structure chart from transform analysis.

After the framework is established, a subhierarchy is created from each second-level module. If the central transform consisted of a single data transformation, the corresponding module need not be changed; if there were several transformations in the central transform, they can be attached as third-level modules, and all data routed through the upper-level module. The creation of the subhierarchies for the afferent and efferent streams is based on the separation of data movement from data transformation. Although the work of moving data is not explicitly represented on a transformation schema, a single transformation with inputs and outputs implicitly represents the moving of each input to the transformation, the carrying out of the transformation, and the moving of each output from the transformation. Figure 9.9 shows the translation of the components of two transformations into separate modules. The representation differs for afferent and efferent transformations; in the former case the mover of the output is the high-level module, and in the latter case the provider of the input is the high-level module. In both cases, the name of the high-level module reflects the job performed by the entire group of modules.

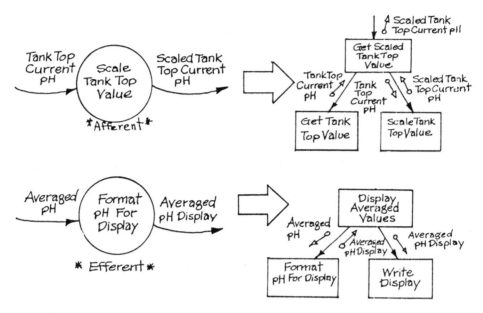

Figure 9.9 Translation of single transformations into structure chart fragments.

When a sequence of two or more transformations are to be converted to a structure chart fragment, there are N+1 levels in the resulting hierarchy, where N is the number of transformations. For an afferent sequence, the mover of the first transformation's output merges with the obtainer of the second transformation's input; for an efferent sequence a similar merging is done. Figure 9.10 shows the structure chart of Figure 9.8 with one afferent and one efferent subhierarchy added; the afferent subhierarchy illustrates the handling of a two-transformation sequence.

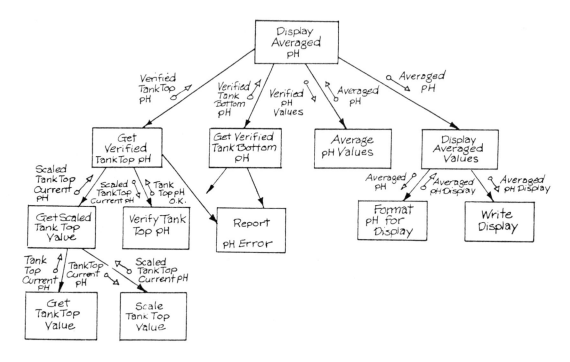

Figure 9.10 Partial structure chart with subhierarchies.

If the transformations of the central transform or of the afferent or efferent streams involve decomposition into parallel components as in Figure 9.6, the translation is somewhat different. Figure 9.11 shows the provider of the ultimate output as a top-level module coordinating the obtaining of the input, the processing of the parallel components, and the reconciliation of the results of component processing.

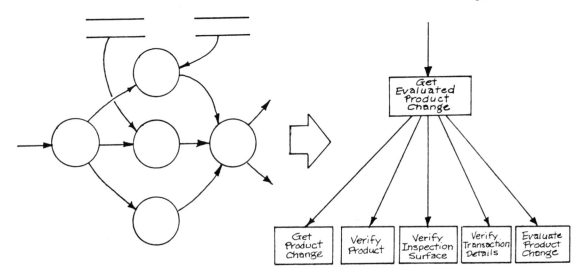

Figure 9.11 Translation of parallel transformations into a structure chart fragment.

The structure charts produced by transform analysis are referred to as *balanced hierarchies*. The term means that:

- the central transform is isolated from the input and output environments by placement in a separate subhierarchy; and

- the highest-level modules are isolated from the low-level details of obtaining data from and sending data to the environment since they see only the net results of low-level module activity.

The transform analysis procedure thus enforces the concept of information hiding, as described in Volume 1, Chapter 4, Modeling Heuristics, and also the separation of essential from implementation details.

9.6 Transaction analysis

The preceding section was restricted to creating the portion of a structure chart corresponding to a single essential model transformation (or the portion of a single transformation assigned to a single task). If several essential model transformations or fragments are assigned to the same task, the structure chart organization must reflect this.

Allocation of several essential transformations to a single task is often necessary because of a time relationship among the essential model pieces (for example, if the required sampling rates are related), or because of task size restrictions. In these cases it is necessary merely to create a module for each essential model fragment, and to subordinate each of these modules to a higher-level coordination module. The high-level module calls the subordinate modules, possibly in an arbitrary order, and enforces any timing relationships such as offsets or activations every other cycle.

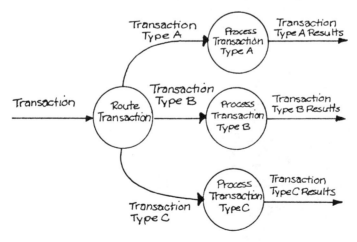

Figure 9.12 A transaction center.

A special case of multiple allocation occurs when several essential model transformations have an input data relationship. Consider the situation illustrated by Figure 9.12, where a transformation accepts an input transaction, checks a "tag," and distributes the output to the appropriate transformation. This structure is referred to as a *transaction center,* and the procedure of constructing the structure chart is called *transaction analysis* [1]. The procedure consists of assigning the identification of type and the routing to a high-level module; modules that obtain the input and that process each type of transaction are called as subordinates, as in Figure 9.13.

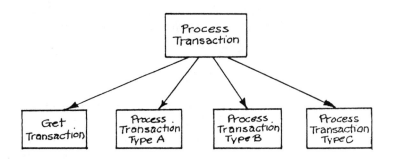

Figure 9.13. Structure chart from transaction analysis.

Transaction and transform analysis may be combined by using transaction analysis to create the top-level superstructure, then using transform analysis to create a subhierarchy for processing each type of transaction. Figure 9.14 shows one of the subhierarchies added to the structure chart from Figure 9.13. Notice that a shared data area has been used to maintain the movement of data "upward" from the afferent processing to the central transform.

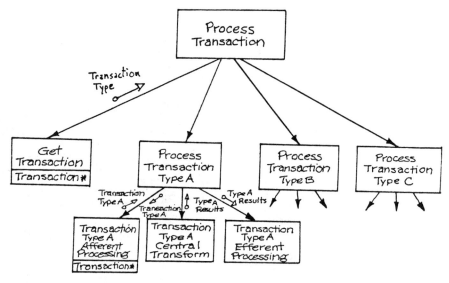

Figure 9.14 Combination of transform and transaction analysis.

9.7 Summary

Good design requires that the portion of a system assigned to a task preserve its organization when transformed into code. The structure chart, which describes the code organization, must thus be created so as not to distort the organization of the transformation schema. The translation techniques introduced in this chapter have as a goal the preservation of this organization.

Chapter 9:References

1.   Meilir Page-Jones, *The Practical Guide to Structured Systems Design.* New York: Yourdon Press, 1980.

10
Structure Chart Refinement

10.1 Introduction

The application of the procedures given in the last chapter will result in a reasonable first-cut structure chart. However, in most cases there are further refinements necessary to produce an optimal code organization. In this chapter we will discuss some criteria for carrying out these refinements. Structure chart modifications leading to design improvements can be discovered by considering the *coupling* of pairs of modules, and the *cohesion, complexity,* and *reusability* of individual modules. A much more detailed treatment of this topic is given in [1].

10.2 Coupling

Modules are coupled because of their interconnections. The connection between two modules may legitimately take the form of a call relationship, of parameters passed between modules, or of a data area shared between modules. It is also possible to couple modules by having one module unconditionally transfer control to another by a "goto." However, this type of coupling violates good design practice and will not be considered here. Using coupling as a refinement technique means examining the coupling between pairs of modules and modifying the structure chart to reduce the extent of coupling where possible. Three possible techniques for reducing coupling are:

- grouping data elements into data structures,

- changing parameters passed through modules that do not use them into shared parameters, and

- eliminating control couples.

Creating data structures from data elements provides a visual simplification of a structure chart, since the reader need follow fewer couples to understand the movement of data among the modules. Data structures may also simplify the code itself, if the implementation language provides facilities for manipulating data structures as units. It is appropriate to use a data structure to make a group of data elements available to a group of modules that need all or most of the elements, as illustrated by Figure 10.1. However, if a data structure is made available to a module that only uses a minority of the data elements, as in Figure 10.2, the module is actually more tightly coupled because of increased exposure to data. The apparent simplicity of passing a complex data structure as a single parameter among modules masks the unnecessary exposure of unneeded data to modules that might inadvertently modify it.

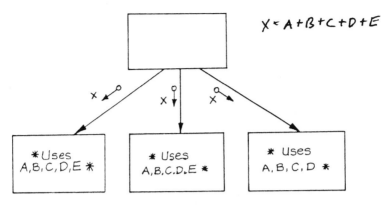

Figure 10.1 Appropriate use of data structure.

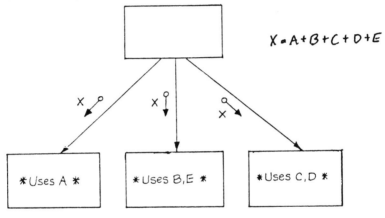

Figure 10.2 Inappropriate use of data structure.

Another consideration in data structure creation is the naturalness of the grouping. The data elements aggregated into the structure should have some relationship in terms of the system's subject matter. A purely arbitrary grouping of elements into a structure (for example, Input Data) doesn't add to the comprehensibility of the structure chart and can mask the unwarranted aggregation of unrelated functions into a single module.

The second technique for improving coupling is the use of shared data areas to reduce unnecessary parameter passing. If a data element or group becomes available in one module and must be used by another module separated from the first, parameter passing leads to the transporting of unused data through the intervening modules, as in Figure 10.3. (The module separation in Figure 10.3 is assumed to be due to the fact that writing x is conditional on decisions made in the intervening modules. If this assumption does not hold, moving the "Write X" module closer to the "Get X" module is a better way of improving the design.) The creation of a data area shared between a small number of modules reduces the overall coupling of such a structure chart, as shown in Figure 10.4. Note that this is a very restrictive use of the idea of a shared data area. Global shared areas, which make all the data available to all the modules, worsen coupling. Sharing a composite data structure among a group of modules that use only a small portions of the structure also constitutes a misuse of the data structure (a shared data area with a number of data elements is a data structure just as is a composite passed parameter).

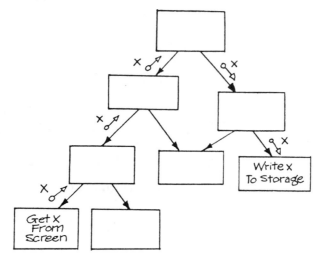

Figure 10.3 Excessive parameter passing.

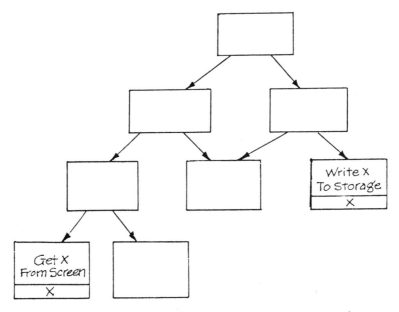

Figure 10.4 Use of shared data area to eliminate parameter passing.

A group of modules sharing a data area can effectively shield the remaining modules in the structure chart from the details of a data storage and manipulation mechanism. Figure 10.5 illustrates such a grouping for the SILLY system (Appendix C). The grouping permits maintenance of up-to-date information about cursor position and format and makes this information accessible and modifiable by means of simple calls.

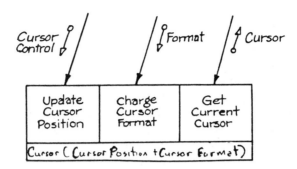

Figure 10.5 An information cluster.

A final criterion for improving coupling is the elimination of control couples. Some control couples, such as those that signal end-of-data and failure to locate stored data are an inevitable part of a hierarchical design and cannot be eliminated. The disguising of control information by the use of special data values, such as high values in a record area to indicate the record was not retrieved, does not reduce control coupling but merely hides it. However, control couples may often be eliminated by:

- placing the execution of an action in the same module as, or close to, the module that senses the condition leading to the action, or

- replacing a called module that receives an activity-directing control couple by two or more simple modules performing atomic activities.

The latter point is illustrated by Figure 10.6. The Display or Transmit Logic States module requires a control couple to decide which function to perform on a particular call. The two individual modules, Display Logic States and Transmit Logic States, on the other hand, require no control input. The decision logic is hidden in the calling module and the interface is thus simplified.

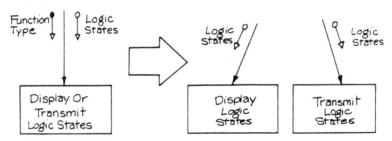

Figure 10.6 Removal of an unnecessary control couple.

Please note that reducing coupling is not an end in itself. Minimizing coupling at the expense of other design criteria may produce a worse overall design.

10.3 Module cohesion

Refinement of a structure chart can be accomplished by investigating the cohesion of individual modules in addition to the coupling of pairs of modules. Cohesion is a measure of the internal unity or relatedness of the components of a module. There are two viewpoints from which to evaluate cohesion, the external viewpoint and the internal viewpoint.

The external cohesion of a module is determined simply by a critical examination of its name — assuming that the name accurately describes the function performed by the module and its subordinates. A module is externally cohesive if its name describes a single function using the system's subject-matter vocabulary. A module's failure to be externally cohesive can thus be due to a name indicating a compound function (for example, a single module for the SILLY system called Update Cursor Position and Change Trigger Word), or to a name that is not subject-matter-specific (for example, Update Stored Data as a module name within SILLY). Note that external cohesion is not a measure of the *partitionability* of a module. A module with many potential subordinate functions, such as Acquire Logic States for the SILLY system, can still perform a single subject-matter-specific job. In fact, a module's external cohesion is the same whether or not it calls upon subordinate modules, since module names summarize the results of a call. External cohesion is a good indicator of the understandability of a module, which in turn will affect its maintainability.

The other viewpoint from which cohesion may be judged is the internal one. Evaluating internal cohesion requires examining the internal structure of a module, which in turn implies that a module specification must be created or obtained. The basic principle is that modules whose elements are related by operating on common data are more cohesive than modules whose elements have merely a time relationship, and that modules of either of the preceding types are more cohesive than modules whose elements belong to some other classification category.

Figure 10.7 shows several modules whose elements are cohesive in a data sense. (We are presuming that the modules are simple enough so that a reader familiar with the case study backgrounds [in Appendices A-D] can construct a satisfactory mental module specification.) Data-related cohesion involves both inherently sequential operations on a data element or composite (Get Current pH might read then scale a sensor value), and also potentially parallel operations such as displaying and transmitting states. Modules containing potentially parallel operations can easily be split into independent, simpler modules and thus are less cohesive. However, all data-related modules have a unity derived from the unity of the data operated on; if this data forms a natural whole from the point of view of the system's subject matter, the module has a corresponding degree of coherence.

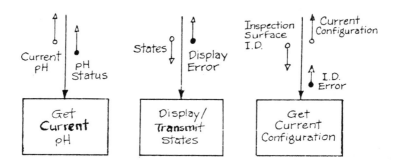

Figure 10.7 Modules with data cohesion.

Figure 10.8 illustrates two modules whose elements have a time rather than a data relationship. Initialize Variables contains a group of actions that "must be done first," and Close Files contains a set of actions that "must be done last." Groupings such as these have inherently poorer cohesiveness than data related modules (notice the unspecific names). What's more, judgments about what must be done first or last are often questionable (variables don't need to be initialized until they are about to be used). The elements of such modules can often be dispersed among other modules to which they have data relationships.

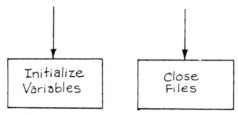

Figure 10.8   Modules with time cohesion.

Modules that are even less cohesive than time-related modules, such as those that lump together "inputs" or "file updates" because they belong to some general data processing category, are so clearly counterproductive that they need no further discussion.

10.4 Module complexity

A module can have high cohesion and simple interfaces to other modules but still be unsatisfactory because of its complexity. In general, a module should be simple enough to be regarded as a single "conceptual unit" for purposes of verification or modification. There is no universally accepted criterion for acceptable complexity, but module size and number of subordinates are useful guidelines. With regard to size, a module that, when coded, produces a listing no longer than one page (or one screen) can be considered small enough. This criterion is based on the idea that having to turn pages or shift screens to see all the logic decreases ease of understanding.

If a module is judged to be too large, it can be simplified by factoring, that is, by identifying portions of logic that can be defined as subordinate modules. A general guideline for factoring is to leave control and coordination logic in the upper-level module, and to assign data manipulations ("number crunching") and input/output operations to lower-level modules. (Based on this criterion, a well-formed structure chart should have modules whose average percentage of control logic is directly proportional to their distance from the bottom.)

The number of other modules called directly from a given module is sometimes called its *fanout*. A module with high fanout (the human short-tern memory limit of seven plus-or-minus two has been proposed as an upper limit) is likely to have complex logic. However, this criterion must be applied with some judgment. A module that uses an index value to select among a group of very similar subordinates has high fanout but a simple logic structure. A group of subordinates of this kind should probably count as a single module for purposes of determining fanout. In the case of a module with excessive fanout, factoring will take the form of defining "subordinate manager" modules that are called from the upper-level module and manage a subset of the original subordinates.

10.5 Module reusability

A final guideline for structure chart refinement is the reusability of individual modules. The guideline applies more to lower-level modules than upper-level modules; the latter are likely to be quite specific in function and difficult to generalize.

A useful measurement for the reusability of a module is its *fan-in*, that is, the number of modules that directly call the module in question. It is important to note that the fan-in of a module is not necessarily the number of callers *within a single structure chart*. A module may be initially defined within the structure chart for one task but find uses within other tasks both within the same system and within other systems. (Whether the reusable module is physically included in each task that uses it, or whether a single system library copy is shared among a group of tasks, is a run-time issue unrelated to the discussion here.) When searching for reusable modules, it is thus important to take a broader view than the task currently being examined.

The factoring process described in the previous section on module complexity is a primary source of reusable modules. In fact, it may be worth factoring modules to look for potential reusability even if the modules are not overly complex. A factored-out module that turns out to be non-reusable can always be reincorporated into its caller.

Reusable modules may perform functions that are quite subject-matter-specific, or they may be generalized to perform functions at a semantic level different from that of the application. Please refer to the discussion of semantic levels and of generalization in Chapter 6, Modeling System Services — Process Management, for more information. When generalizing to create a reusable module, it is important to remember that reusability is only one of the criteria for structure chart quality. Providing a reusable module that has an overly complex interface or that has poor cohesion will not improve the overall quality of a structure chart.

10.6 Summary

The reusability and maintainability of a task is largely dependent on the organization of the modules from which it is constructed There are a number of criteria by which the quality of a task's module structure can be judged. This chapter has presented the criteria of intermodule coupling, module cohesion, module complexity, and module reusability, and has suggested modifications that can be made to a task's module structure (represented by a structure chart) to improve quality based on these criteria.

Chapter 10: References

1. Meiler Page-Jones. *The Practical Guide to Structured Systems Design.* New York: Yourdon Press, 1980.

Section 4

Before and Beyond
the Implementation Model

The two chapters of the final section examine the connections between the implementation model and the preceding and succeeding stages of development.

Chapter 11, Sizing, Efficiency, and Optimization, discusses the connection between the guidelines for creating an optimum implementation and the more specific techniques involved in performance improvement.

Chapter 12, Implementation Model Traceability, describes methods for documenting the connections between an implementation model and the essential model from which it was derived.

11
Sizing, Efficiency, and Optimization

11.1 Introduction

We stated in the first chapter of Volume 1 that real-time system development need no longer be implementation-dominated, but instead should be driven by the problem to be solved. Implicit in this statement is the idea that implementation resources are available in sufficient quantities and at low enough prices to allow an implementation to be built with relatively low distortion of the problem. Most real-time systems have stringent timing constraints that must be met for the system to be effective; but we have asserted that often the order of the expected resources required is less than the order of the resources available so that we may indeed focus mainly on the problem to be solved.

Nevertheless, there are situations in which there is difficulty in reaching an acceptable approximation to required behavior with a proposed implementation. Before implementation resources are committed, we need to be able to judge with reasonable confidence whether a proposed implementation will satisfy the constraints. We stated in Chapter 2, Identifying Implementation Constraints, that constraints were in fact *quantifiable*. An implementation model describes in a qualitative way the use of the chosen resources; the problem that remains is to estimate *quantitative resource usage*. Should we anticipate insufficient resources for the work to be done, we must reorganize the model, or assign more resources to a particular unit of the implementation.

This chapter addresses the problems of sizing a proposed implementation, and describes techniques for reorganizing the implementation should the developed system fail to be implementable within the chosen resources or fail a performance test.

11.2 Identifying resource usage

The implementation model shows what processing must be done and what data must be stored by each processor and task. Each processor is capable of executing a limited number of instructions in a specified time and has available only a limited amount of primary memory.

There are further limits to resource availability within a processor. A single task, for example, may not be permitted to address more than a certain amount of memory; there may be limits on the number of active tasks, and so on. To convince ourselves that a proposed implementation will be satisfactory, it is therefore necessary to identify available resources and any limits imposed on their use; if *for any resource* usage is greater than availability, then the implementation will fail.

Resource usage estimations are necessarily global — they must cover all the resources used by all tasks within a processor. The tasks described by the implementation model are not all active at a given point in time, and so an implementation will be potentially acceptable if the memory required at any one instant is never greater than that available, and the processing power required over any interval is less than processing power available.

As a result, the job of estimating resource usage can be very large. We may reduce the problem by ignoring those resources where availability is large or easily expandable. Estimates need only be precise enough to show that a particular resource is unlikely to be overused. For those areas in which there is doubt as to the viability of the implementation it is necessary to run tests to find out exactly how much memory or processing time is used; this may be an opportunity to begin implementation on portions of the system thought to be relatively stable. In this section, we focus on how we might examine the usage of three kinds of resource: memory, processing time usage, and response time.

Memory within a processor is used by several identifiable components: the operating system, shared data areas, and active tasks. The size of the operating system that is always in memory can be obtained from the vendor; any memory used only when required should be regarded as a part of the task that causes the memory usage. To estimate the size of shared data areas, the size and number of occurrences of each field in the entity-relationship diagram allocated to this processor and held in main memory must be known, together with any additional data used as pointers. The memory size of all the active tasks at an instant is made up of shared reentrant code (which should be counted only once, regardless of the number of the tasks that use it), together with the code used exclusively by each of the active tasks. This computation tells us the instantaneous memory usage of all the active tasks together; as tasks acquire or give up memory for local data use, or "overlay" code, the memory usage of a task may change. In more sophisticated processors, physical memory may be swapped between active tasks one page at a time rather than swapping in and out of the entire task. This of course increases the amount of memory that is perceived to be available at the cost of both processor time (to execute the swap) and response time (to retrieve the memory from secondary storage).

Required processing time for a task may be estimated by adding the times required to process continuous and discrete data and to run the system software that services the task over a specified interval. Only the CPU active time attributable to the task should be included in the estimate; time waiting for I/O or running and servicing other tasks should be excluded, as shown in Figure 11.1. The time needed to process inputs into outputs over an interval is the time needed to process a single packet multiplied by the number of packets that arrive over the interval. For continuous data, the number of packets is determined by the sampling rate. For discrete data, the maximum expected number of arrivals over the interval (the *burst rate*) should be computed. This can then be used to compute the *maximum utilization* of the processor over the interval. Finally, the time needed for each context switch must be added to the total. If we assume that each task finishes its processing without interruption, then there are two switches for each task that runs in response to the arrival of a flow (whether sampled or arriving discretely). Note that the arrival of a second discrete flow while a task is operating will allow the task to pick up the flow without giving up control, thus *reducing* the number of switches required. The arrival of a flow that is processed by a higher priority task will cause two switches (one to the higher priority task, and one out of it) which is no worse than assuming that the lower priority task finishes its job before the next packet. To find the worst case, therefore, the highest rate of arrival of flows that permits the receiving task to switch momentarily to a background task must be found.

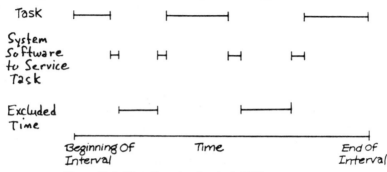

Figure 11.1 Time line showing task CPU usage.

The response time for the processing of a particular essential model event may be estimated by following the active flow through the tasks that execute the response. The total processing time for the event is the sum of the processing time for each task that processes the flow together with the switching time between the tasks. However, it is also possible for a higher priority task to interrupt the processing. For any (enabled) response, the time for portions of other enabled responses that execute in higher priority tasks (plus the necessary switching time) should also be added. In addition, if several events may occur in rapid succession, queuing time must be taken into account.

As can be seen from the previous discussions, the total number of combinations can be very large. It is simply not possible to check all possibilities; judgment must be exercised to decide which of the many options to check rigorously. Nevertheless, using the model to evaluate the rough costs of a particular configuration can help avoid constructing a system with processing requirement orders of magnitude larger than the resources available.

11.3 Estimates and reality

Once the system has been implemented, we may find that estimates for resource usage and response time were inaccurate, leading to a system that does not meet its constraints. This can be discovered by running performance tests for time-critical portions of the system or by examining actual memory usage. The failure of a specific performance test indicates a need to reexamine resource availability and usage for the *one resource* that is in short supply.

At this stage in the development process it may still be possible to acquire more resources; the system can then be retested without further change. However, it may be necessary to *optimize* the code to reduce memory usage or to increase the speed of time-critical sections. Typically, such change in the system increases the distortion of the essential model and is not to be recommended; optimization should be limited to the portion of the system that failed a performance test, and should cease once the system meets its constraints. This plan of attack limits distortion to a relatively small part of the whole system. Note that this is quite different from the more traditional approach to optimization, in which the entire system is subject to distortion in the name of efficiency. A machine-efficient implementation of a system is a worthy goal since the unit hardware costs can be reduced; however, the distortion introduced will cause higher maintenance bills. Machine-efficiency increases in importance when many copies of a system are to be produced; reducing hardware costs for a system to be installed in every traffic signal in the country is much more valuable than for a "one-off" control system implementation.

Given that resource availability is fixed, and that optimization is required, the implemented system must first be examined to find out which portion of the system can be optimized effectively. It has been our experience that guesswork in this area is uniformly inaccurate. System utilities can be constructed that collect data each clock cycle for later examination. These utilities may operate at the processor level (noting which task is active each cycle) or at the task level (noting the address of the next executable instruction within a single chosen task.) This data can provide valuable insights into where time is being spent. It is not unusual to discover that code that should not be executed is being run, and even to find bugs. (In one task under optimization it was found that a counter was being used incorrectly, causing a portion of code to be executed 64K - n times rather than n times!)

Once the problem has been identified, optimization can begin to reduce the use of the critical resource.

11.4 Optimization techniques

Optimization is the act of *reducing* or *redistributing* the use of a specific resource in response to the failure of a performance test. We shall examine failures in instantaneous memory usage, the use of processing time, and response time.

An instantaneous requirement for more memory than is available calls for either a reduction in memory usage or spreading the use of available memory over time. Memory usage may be reduced by reorganizing memory to find a more compact representation of the same data; for example, packing several bits or bytes into a word. Typically, this then increases the time taken to access and update data items. Other methods are to recompute data items when needed rather than store intermediate values, or to apply a more compact algorithm to reduce code size. Care must be exercised not to write more words of code than are saved in data space. Memory usage may be spread over time by redistributing code and data between shared and private areas. For example, shared reentrant modules will reduce instantaneous memory usage if several tasks use the shared modules during the critical interval. However, the shared modules may still occupy memory even when not in use. If modules are only used at certain times they may be overlayed so that only modules in use actually occupy memory; there is a time trade-off here since it takes processor time to swap code in and out of primary memory. The same principles apply for shared data items. Data shared only by a few tasks may be passed between the tasks at run-time, or the tasks may be replaced by a single larger task.

Processing time may be reduced by three basic methods: finding a faster algorithm, trading off speed for memory, or code-level reexpression. The first technique, in the mathematical arena, is the subject of research papers whose results are often available from collections of algorithms published by professional societies. The same is often true for algorithms specifically for data processing functions — searching, sorting, and the like. However, the specific characteristics of the problem at hand may have a significant impact on the usefulness of a particular algorithm. For example, a slow searching algorithm may be more effective than the theoretically faster algorithm if the data to be searched has certain characteristics; a linear search may be faster than a binary search if frequently accessed items can be placed at the head of the search list. Speed of data access may also be increased by reorganizing memory into units more easily accessed by the processor. Less code will need to be executed for each access if the data is organized into words or bytes, though this often will use more memory. A final technique for reducing processing time is the global re-expression of frequently executed portions of code into a more efficient form. Examples include the replacement of calls to data access modules by inline code, thus obviating the need for a subroutine call; replacement of high-level language module calling mechanisms by simpler versions that do not check types or the number of parameters; and the replacement of generalized data access by precompilation of data names into pointers as described in Chapter 7, Modeling System Services — Data Management. The same technique can be applied locally by rewriting time-critical modules in a more efficient programming language, typically an assembly language.

The techniques for improving response time rely heavily on the techniques for reducing processing time. Meeting response time requirements forces the developer to execute all the code needed to produce an output on receipt of an input as rapidly as possible. In many cases, however, not all of the response has to be executed to produce an output and code may be removed from the time-critical portion of a response. Consider a continuously operating transformation that must produce a specific continuous output from two continuous inputs at a certain rate; the rate at which the inputs vary may not be the same, leading to an implementation in which the input that varies more slowly does not have computations performed on it every cycle. This is a specific application of the techniques described in Chapter 4, Task Modeling; the slower portion of the response has been factored out of the control loop. Slow response to an operator also has a psychological component: two short waits are preferred to a single longer wait. Operators often require some positive feedback that the computer system has received a command; if the computation to be performed is relatively long, the response may be reorganized to interleave data input with computation and to provide feedback as computation proceeds. While the total response time may remain the same, the perceived waiting time is reduced.

11.5 Summary

Efficiency is an economic issue. Trade-offs between machine efficiency and the efficiency of the use of both developers and maintainers on the project occur as implementation proceeds. Optimization may be required as a last resort to meet performance constraints.

12
Implementation Model Traceability

12.1 Introduction

Chapter 7 of Volume 2, Essential Model Traceability, justified the need for traceability between the narrative specification document, the environmental model and the behavioral model. A tool for keeping the traces, namely tracing tables, was described. The same need exists to trace the implementation model back to its sources. The implementation model is *derived* from the essential model, so implementation model traceability is intended to answer two questions: First, is each essential model component implemented by the implementation model? Second, is each implementation model component required to implement some essential model component? Tracing tables can again be used to show the connections between the models.

The production of the implementation model is often supported by a narrative document that describes the implementation constraints on the design. Please note that the implementation model is *not* derived from this document in the same way that the essential model is built from the narrative specification document. Instead the implementation constraints place *limits* on the possible solutions that may be *evaluated* against the constraints as described in Chapter 11 — Sizing, Efficiency, and Optimization. This is a part of the act of building the model, rather than a static correlation between components such as that shown by tracing tables.

12.2 Tracing implementation model components

The implementation model is a coherent whole which is built in three stages; each stage contains essential model responses or fragments of responses. In some cases, there is a one-to-one correspondence between an implementation unit and an essential model response. In other words, a processor, task, or module implements a single, entire essential response. In these cases, the tracing table entry should be created at the level of the correspondence. Otherwise, the tracing should be done at the lowest implementation model level. To illustrate this let us examine the Cruise Control System (described in Appendix A). This system does not have structure charts built for its tasks since each task is relatively simple; the lower levels of the model for each task represent the fragments of essential model responses. (If a structure chart had been built, each fragment would correspond to a leg of the chart.)

Table 1 shows a partial tracing table for Monitor Engine, Control Learning, and Report Speed. The left-hand column is used to define the implementation unit under examination; the right-hand column contains the names (and numbers) of the essential model responses embodied by the entry to the left. Note that several entries appear in the essential response column when several responses are packaged into a single implementation unit. Similarly, since fragmentation of the responses may occur, a single essential model response may be referenced several times.

Task Segment	Source In Essential Model
1.1 Control Engine Monitoring, Learning and Speed Reporting.	1. - Monitor Engine 2.1 - Determine Mode Of Operation 2.3.1 - Control Learning Mode
1.2 -- Set Accumulate Rotations Flag.	Enable From 2.3.1 -- Control Learning Mode To 2.3.2 -- Accumulate Rotations.
1.3 Reset Accumulate Rotations & Flag.	Disable From 2.3.1 -- Control Learning Mode To 2.3.2 -- Accumulate Rotations
1.4 -- Set Conversion Factor	2.3.3 Set Conversion Factor
1.5 Reset Report Current Speed Flag	Disable From 2.1 -- Determine Mode Of Operation To 2.4 -- Report Current Speed
1.6 -- Set Report Current Speed Flag.	Enable From 2.1 -- Determine Mode Of Operation To 2.4 -- Report Current Speed

Table 12.1.

Table 1 may be inverted so as to index from the essential model responses as shown in Table 2.

Essential Model Transformation/Flow	Destination In Implementation Model
1. -- Monitor Engine	1.1 -- Control Engine Monitoring, Learning, and Speed Reporting.
2.1 -- Determine Mode Of Operation	1.1 -- Control Engine Monitoring, Learning and Speed Reporting.
Enable From 2.1 To 2.4 -- Report Speed	1.6 -- Set Report Current Speed Flag
Disable From 2.1 To 2.4 -- Report Current Speed	1.5 -- Reset Report Current Speed Flag.
2.3.1 -- Control Learning Mode	1.1 -- Control Engine Monitoring, Learning and Speed Reporting
Enable From 2.3.1 To 2.3.2 -- Accumulate Rotation	1.2 -- Set Accumulate Rotations Flag.
Disable From 2.3.1 To 2.3.2 -- Accumulate Rotations	1.3 -- Reset Accumulated Rotations and Flag.
2.3.3 -- Set Conversion Factor	1.4 -- Set Conversion Factor

Table 12.2.

12.3 Tracing for system services

System services exist in order to carry out functions *required by the implementation.* For example, a data transmission network exists only to transmit data between processors; choosing to have several processors in a design is its justification. Any additional models of system utilities built to support an implementation should have a statement of purpose just as with other essential models. In this case, however, the reason for the system is the needs of the implementation of the application.

System services may carry out essential model functions by providing general support for implementation technology or more directly by virtue of their use by the application code. In the latter case, the implementation model for the application will contain a reference to the use of the service utility. These connections are modeled as described in Chapter 6, Modeling System Services — System Software.

12.4 Summary

An implementation model is intended to have the same behavior as the essential model from which it is derived. To help guarantee this, it is useful to trace the essential model responses to their implementation model counterparts and vice-versa. Tracing tables satisfy this need.

Appendix A
Cruise Control System

TABLE OF CONTENTS

Implementation Resources

The cruise control system is to be implemented on a single powerful microprocessor with 16 interrupts which shall be connected to the control signals that come from the driver's console.

The system software for the chosen microprocessor permits several (up to 8) tasks to run simultaneously, and it has the capability to schedule tasks on a timer to a resolution of 10 milliseconds. The operating system and the interrupt handler each count as a single task. The operating system occupies 16K bytes of memory; each task may occupy up to 16K bytes. However, the total memory of the system is only 64K bytes which must be shared among the tasks, including the operating system and the interrupt handler. There is also provision for a single data area which can be shared among all tasks; there is no shared code capability.

The microprocessor can execute one million instructions per second; the code for context switching between tasks is 400 instructions long.

Transformation Schemas

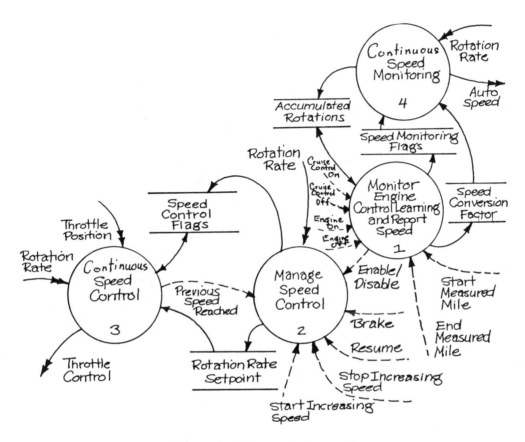

Figure A.0 Cruise control microprocessor.

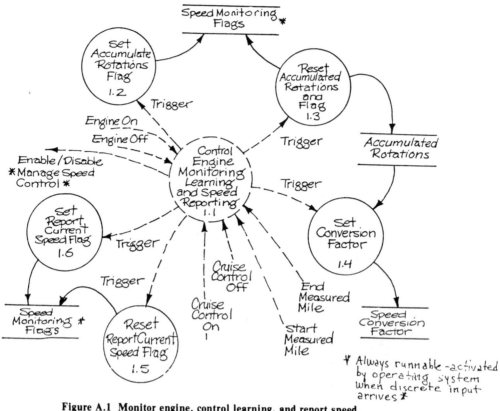

Figure A.1 Monitor engine, control learning, and report speed.

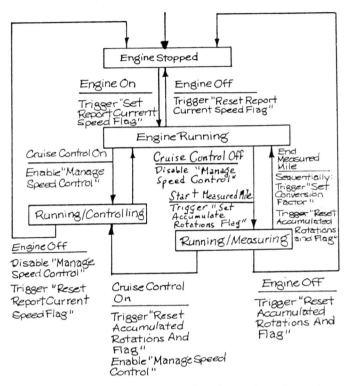

Figure A.1.1 Control engine monitoring, learning, and speed reporting.

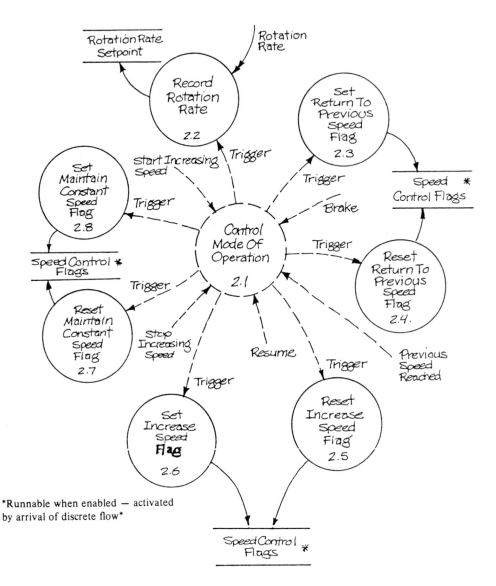

*Runnable when enabled — activated
by arrival of discrete flow*

Figure A.2 Manage speed control.

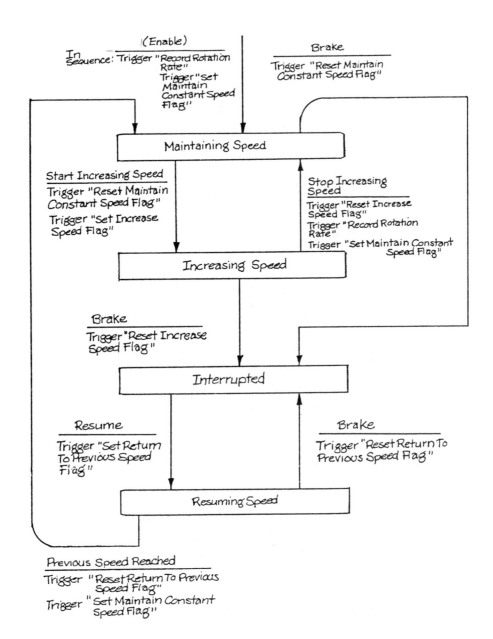

Figure A.2.1 Control mode of operation.

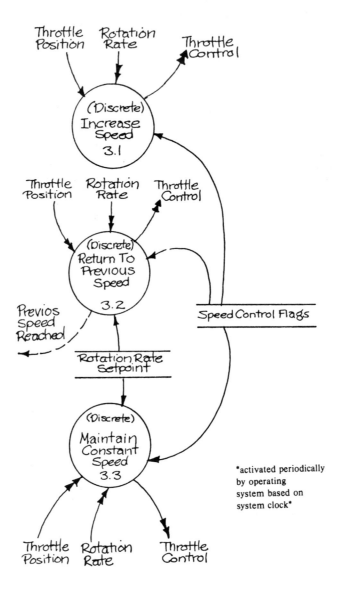

Figure A.3 Continuous speed control.

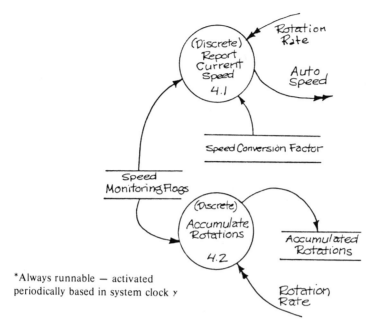

*Always runnable — activated
periodically based in system clock y

Figure A.4 Continuous speed monitoring.

Data Dictionary

accumulate rotations flag	=	**
		values : [true | false]
increase speed flag	=	**
		values: [true | false]
maintain constant speed flag	=	**
		* values: [true | false]*
report current speed flag	=	**
		values : [true | false]
return to previous speed flag	=	**
		= *values : [true | false]*
speed control flags	=	*flags to manage periodic speed control*
	=	return to previous speed flag + increase speed flag + maintain constant speed flag
speed monitoring flags	=	*flags to manage periodic speed monitoring*
	=	accumulate rotations flag + report current speed flag

Transformation Specifications

1.2 Set Accumulate Rotations Flag

Precondition

> None

Postcondition

> ACCUMULATE ROTATIONS FLAG = TRUE

1.3 Reset Accumulate Rotations and Flag

Precondition

> None

Postcondition

> ACCUMULATED ROTATIONS = 0
>
> ACCUMULATED ROTATIONS FLAG = FALSE

1.4 Set Conversion Factor

Precondition

> None

Postcondition

> SPEED CONVERSION FACTOR = ACCUMULATED ROTATIONS

1.5 Reset Report Current Speed Flag

Precondition

> None

Postcondition

> REPORT CURRENT SPEED FLAG = FALSE

1.6 Set Report Current Speed Flag

Precondition

> None

Postcondition

> REPORT CURRENT SPEED FLAG = TRUE

2.2. Record Rotation Rate

Precondition

> None

Postcondition

> ROTATION RATE in ROTATION RATE SETPOINT

2.3 Set Return to Previous Speed Flag

Precondition

> None

Postcondition

> RETURN TO PREVIOUS SPEED FLAG = TRUE

2.4 Reset Return to Previous Speed Flag

Precondition

> None

Postcondition

> RETURN TO PREVIOUS SPEED FLAG = FALSE

2.5 Reset Increase Speed Flag

Precondition

None

Postcondition

INCREASE SPEED FLAG = FALSE

2.6 Set Increase Speed Flag

Precondition

None

Postcondition

INCREASE SPEED FLAG = TRUE

2.7 Reset Maintain Constant Speed

Precondition

None

Postcondition

MAINTAIN CONSTANT SPEED FLAG = FALSE

2.8 Set Maintain Constant Speed Flag

Precondition

None

Postcondition

MAINTAIN CONSTANT SPEED = TRUE

3.1 (Discrete) Increase Speed

Precondition 1

> THROTTLE POSITION < 80% of max.

and   INCREASE SPEED FLAG set

Postcondition 1

> Instantaneous rate of increase per second of ROTATION RATE maintained at 2% ± .25% of current value of ROTATION RATE

Precondition 2

> THROTTLE POSITION at ⩾ 80% of max.

and   INCREASE SPEED FLAG set

Postcondition 2

> Instantaneous rate of increase per second of ROTATION RATE maintained at 0

3.2 (Discrete) Return to Previous Speed

Precondition 1

> RETURN TO PREVIOUS SPEED FLAG set

and   time since flag set ⩽ 0.5 sec.

Postcondition 1

> Match THROTTLE CONTROL to THROTTLE POSITION

Precondition 2

> RETURN TO PREVIOUS SPEED FLAG set

and   time since flag set > 0.5 sec.

Postcondition 2

Maintain rate of increase per second of ROTATION RATE
at 0.1* (ROTATION RATE SETPOINT - ROTATION RATE)

3.3 (Discrete) Maintain Constant Speed

Precondition 1

MAINTAIN CONSTANT SPEED FLAG set

and   ROTATION RATE within 1% of ROTATION RATE SETPOINT

and   time since flag set ≤ 0.5 sec.

Postcondition 1

Match THROTTLE CONTROL to THROTTLE POSITION

Precondition 2

MAINTAIN CONSTANT SPEED FLAG set

and   ROTATION RATE within 1% of ROTATION RATE SETPOINT

and   time since flag set > 0.5 sec.

Postcondition 2

Maintain ROTATION RATE within 1% of ROTATION RATE SETPOINT

4.1 (Discrete) Report Current Speed

Precondition 1

REPORT CURRENT SPEED FLAG is set

Postcondition 1

AUTO SPEED = ROTATION RATE/(SPEED CONVERSION FACTOR * 3600)

4.2 (Discrete) Accumulate Rotations

Precondition 1

ACCUMULATE ROTATIONS FLAG is SET

Postcondition 1

ACCUMULATED ROTATIONS = ACCUMULATED ROTATIONS
+ ROTATION RATE $^*\triangle$T

Appendix B
Bottle Filling System

TABLE OF CONTENTS

Implementation Resources

Background

The system is to be implemented using a pair of microprocessors. One (the Equipment Control Processor) will perform the closed-loop control functions such as controlling vat level and pH, and will also monitor and operate the mechanical equipment such as the labeler and the bottle release mechanism. The other processor (the User Interface Processor) will accept and process keyboard input from the line operators and the area supervisor, and will produce screen displays for Line Status and Area Status.

There will be a set of interrupt lines between the processors; in other words, either processor will be able to cause an external interrupt to the other by issuing a command. In addition, there will be a standard data communications line between the processors cabable of transmitting messages. The "handshaking" relating to the D.C. line will be handled by system software. An application task in either processor need only set up a message buffer and request transmission. The completion of transmission will generate a software interrupt in the receiving processor, with the message stored in a buffer accessible to application tasks.

Each processor will be supplied with an operating system capable of managing an optional background task and a set of interrupt-activated tasks. There are three types of interrupts; external, software, and system clock. An interrupt of one of the first two types will cause control to be transferred to the application task associated with the interrupt. A system clock interrupt causes a lookup in a user-supplied table, which specifies task activations in terms of offset and frequency. For example, the table entries 1,5,A and 2,10,B specify that the first clock interrupt after startup and every fifth interrupt thereafter will activate A, and that the second clock interrupt after startup and every tenth thereafter will activate B.

The interrupt-activated tasks themselves may be interrupted, but not by the same type of interrupt that activated the task; in other words, the handling of an interrupt must be completed before another of the same type is honored. When the last outstanding interrupt-activated task reports completion, control is transferred to the background task, if there is one, until the next interrupt; otherwise, the operating system idles.

Transformation Schemas and Structure Charts

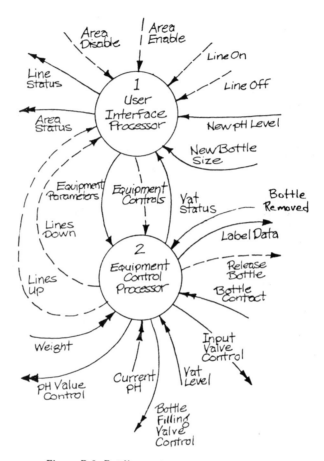

Figure B.0 Bottling system processors.

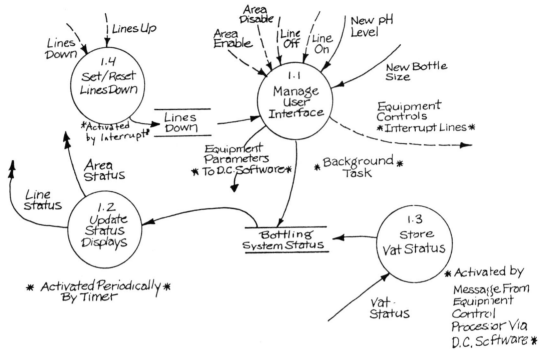

Figure B.1 User interface processor.

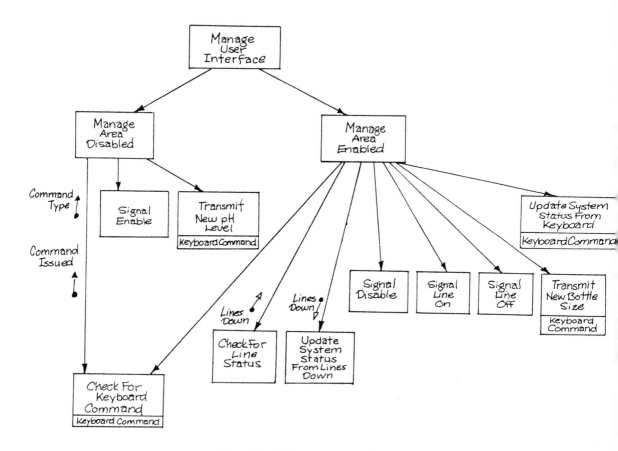

Figure B.1.1 Manage user interface.

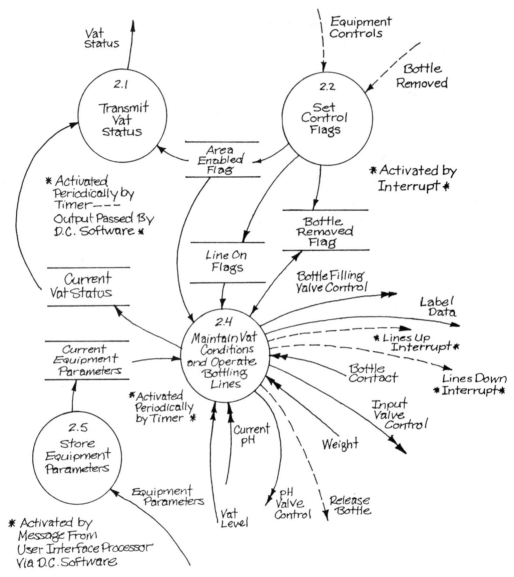

Figure B.2 Equipment control processor.

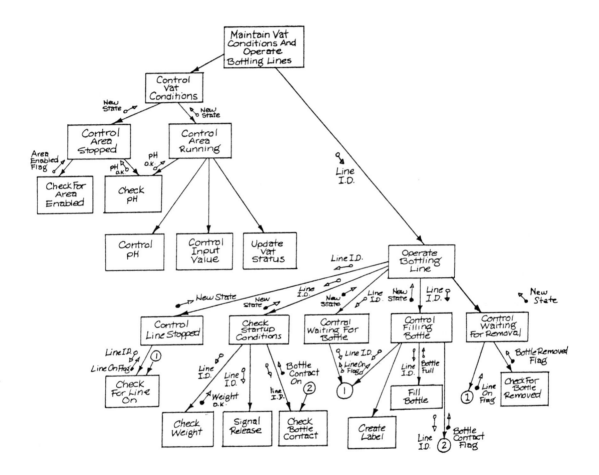

Figure B.2.4 Maintain vat conditions and operate bottling lines.

Data Dictionary

area enabled flag   =   *values: [yes | no]*

bottle contact on   =   *values: [yes | no]*

bottle full flag   =   *values: [yes | no]*

bottle removed flag   =   *values: [yes | no]*

bottling system status =   vat status + [area is off | area is on] +
      {line status}

command issued   =   *values: [yes | no]*

command type   =   *values: [area enabled | area disabled | line on |
      line off | new pH | new size]*

current equipment parameters = equipment parameters

current vat status   =   vat status

cycle time flag   =   *values: [yes | no]*

equipment controls   =   [line on | line off | area enable | area disable]

equipment parameters =   [new pH level | new bottle size]

keyboard command   =   [area enabled | area disabled | new pH level |
      {line number + [line on | line off | new bottle size}]

lines down   =   *values: [yes | no]*

line on flag   =   *values: [yes | no]*

line on flags   =   {line id + line on flag}

lines up   =   *values: [yes | no]*

pH ok   =   *values: [yes | no]*

weight ok   =   *values: [yes | no]*

Appendix C
SILLY System
(Science and Industry Little Logic Yzer*)

TABLE OF CONTENTS

Original author: John Shuttleworth, N.V. Philips

Implementation Resources

Now that we have some ideas of what this SILLY thing is to do, let's concentrate on working out the construction details.

Obviously, one of the major concerns is the user interface. The attached picture of the keyboard layout (Figure C.KB) contains some notes about specific key functions, display formats, etc., which should be useful although not necessarily complete. The keyboard, by the way, is on a five-by-six grid (five output lines and six input lines).

Another major issue is the hardware configuration. We have some components already in stock which we would like incorporated into the completed layout. One component is the microprocessor-plus-memory setup shown on the attached block diagram (Figure C.MP). It has a one-megahertz speed, and in addition to the four external interrupt connections has a programmable timer facility which can be used to generate internal interrupts at multiples of one millisecond. The address space is broader than the PROM and RAM; in other words, other memories may be connected to the bus structure, and the micro can treat them as part of its overall memory.

Another component we would like used is a dot-matrix display, 256 bits wide and 128 bits high. This display has no internal memory and must be refreshed continually on a bit-by-bit basis.

Other than that, the hardware configuration is unconstrained — just keep it cheap!

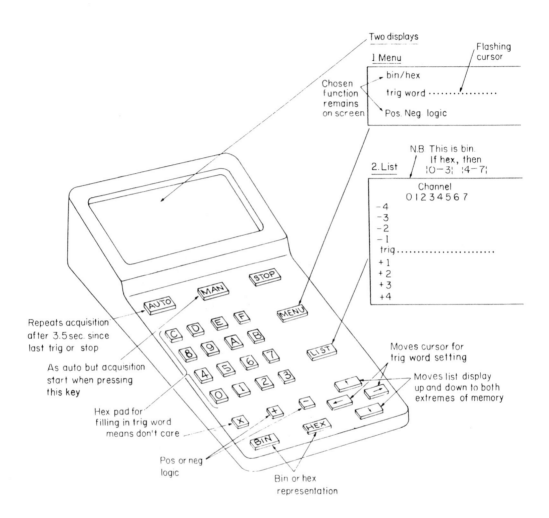

Figure C.KB. Keyboard layout.

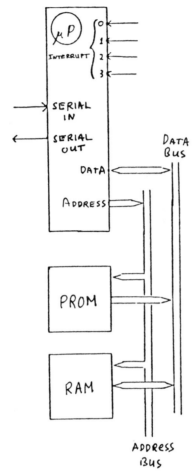

Figure C.MP. **Micrcoprocessor-plus-memory setup.**

Transformation Schemas and Structure Charts

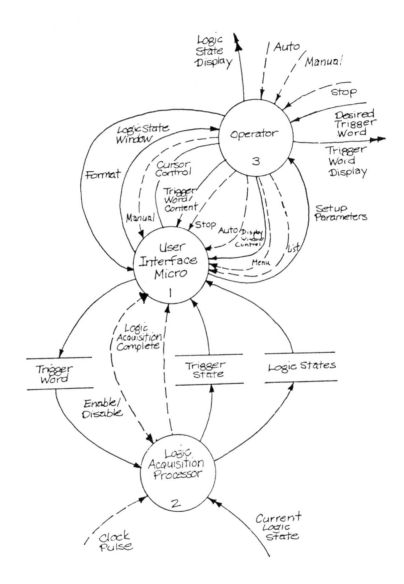

Figure C.O SILLY processor configuration.

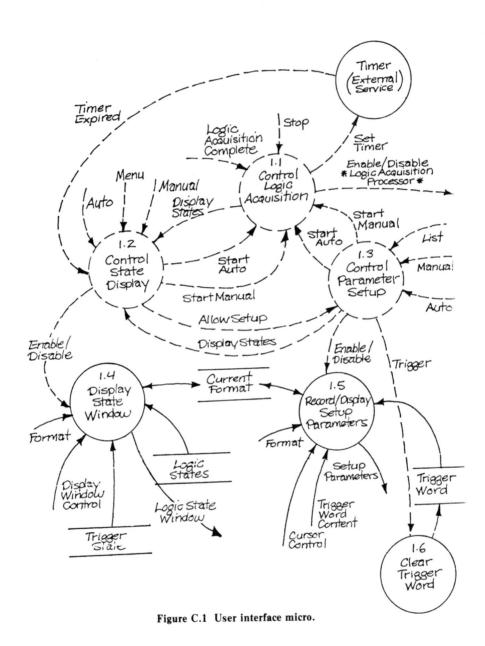

Figure C.1 User interface micro.

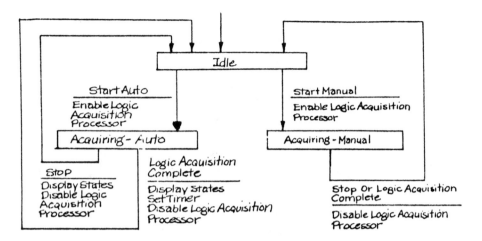

Figure C.1.1 Control logic acquisition.

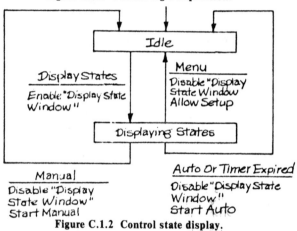

Figure C.1.2 Control state display.

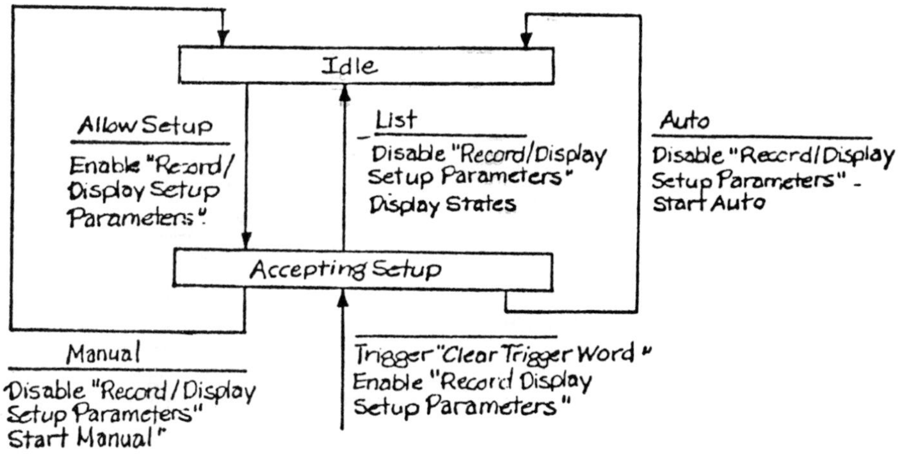

Figure C.1.3 Control parameter setup.

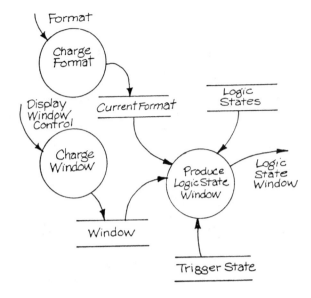

Figure C.1.4 Display state window.

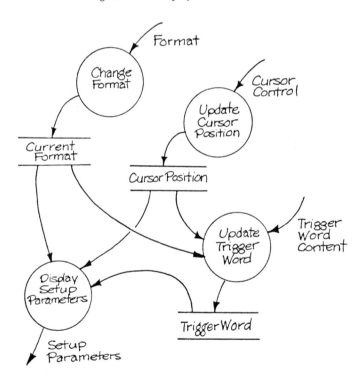

Figure C.1.5 Record display setup parameter.

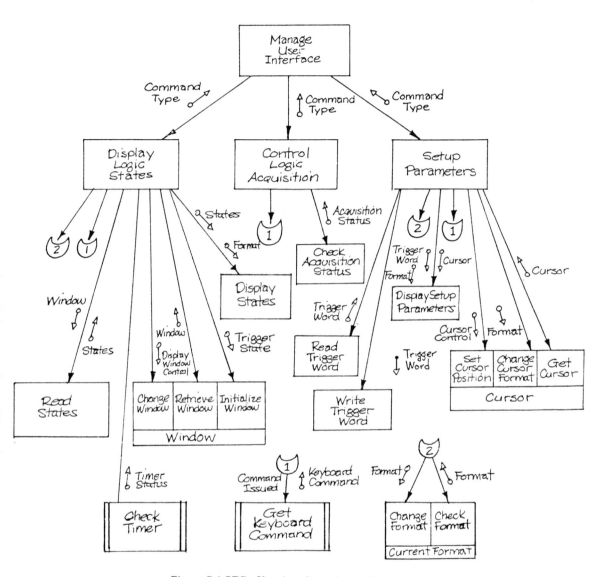

Figure C.1.STC. User interface micro task structure.

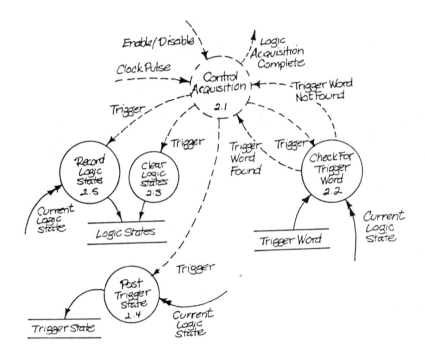

Figure C.2 Logic acquisition processor.

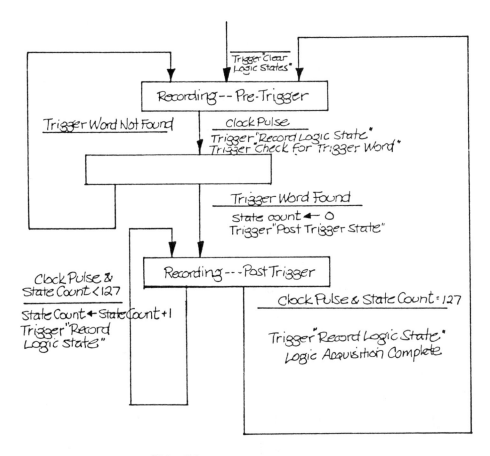

Figire C.2.1 Control acquisition.

Data Dictionary

allow setup	= **
current format	= **
	= format
cursor control	= *control keys to move cursor*
	= *values: [LEFT ARROW | RIGHT ARROW]*
cursor position	= **
display states	= **
display window control	= *control keys to change display window
	= *values: [UPARROW | DOWNARROW]*
format	= * control keys to set desired format of displays*
	= *values: [BIN | HEX]*
list	= * control key to switch display mode*
logic acquisition complete	= **
logic state window	= *logic state display that fits onto screen

form : two forms exist; in the binary form, the value of each level for each channel, ordered from 7 to 0, is displayed; in hexadecimal form, the value of level for channels 7-4 and 3-0 is displayed as hexadecimal digits

= { 8 { channel + level } 8 } 8

menu	= * control key to switch display mode*
set timer	= **
setup parameters	= * see Figure C.D.1 for setup Parameter Screen*
start auto	= **
start manual	= **
trigger expired	= **

trigger word context   = *specified value of desired trigger word*

*form: two forms exist; in the binary form, '0,' '1'
and '?' are accepted to set the match level of each channel
from 1 to 8; in the hexadecimal form, '0' to '9,' 'A' to
'F' and '?' are accepted to set the match level for channels
1-4 and 5-8*

window   = *state number of state displayed in center of logic state

=   window*

= state number

Transformation Specifications

1.4 Display State Window

Local term: WINDOW: set to TRIGGER STATE on enable

Precondition 1

FORMAT occurs

Postcondition 1

CURRENT FORMAT = FORMAT

Produce LOGIC STATE WINDOW

Precondition 2

DISPLAY WINDOW CONTROL occurs

Postcondition 2

change window

Produce LOGIC STATE WINDOW

1.4.1 Change Window

if   (DISPLAY WINDOW CONTROL = UPARROW) & (WINDOW < 255-4) then

WINDOW ← WINDOW + 1

if   (DISPLAY WINDOW CONTROL = DOWNARROW) & (WINDOW > 0 = 3) then

WINDOW ← WINDOW − 1

1.4.2 Produce Logic State Window

select the states of LOGIC STATES between WINDOW +4 and WINDOW − 3

Display the states in FORMAT

1.6 Clear Trigger Word

Precondition

None

Postcondition

TRIGGER WORD is null

Appendix D
Defect Inspection System

TABLE OF CONTENTS

Implementation Resources

The computer configuration for the Defect Inspection System has a minicomputer to manage the interactions between the supervisor and the inspection surfaces and two microcomputers each managing two surfaces each. The supervisor will be provided with a single graphics terminal which is driven from the Product Management Minicomputer. This terminal will be used to change sheet sizes, the configuration, and the product standards for each surface. The computer is equipped with a hard disk and has two links to the microcomputers. A microcomputer controls the inspection surfaces monitored by a single operator. The start and stop buttons for each surface are a part of the control panel for each micro, but the signals are wired directly into the Product Management Computer. A link to the Product Management minicomputer is also provided. Figure D-BKG shows the overall configuration.

The software environment for the micro allows up to four tasks, none of which may be bigger than 32 Kb. A shared global memory area is available to all tasks. Tasks may wait on interrupts after activation, and may use an operating system service "Activate Task" to initiate other tasks in the system. The total memory for the micro is 128 Kb including the operating system, shared global memory area, and all tasks.

The minicomputer is capable of running any number of tasks, though only four may be resident in memory at any one time. Tasks may be swapped out of memory when not in use.

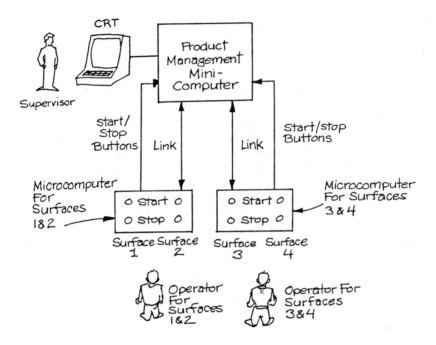

Figure D.BKG Overall hardware configuration.

Schematic Diagrams

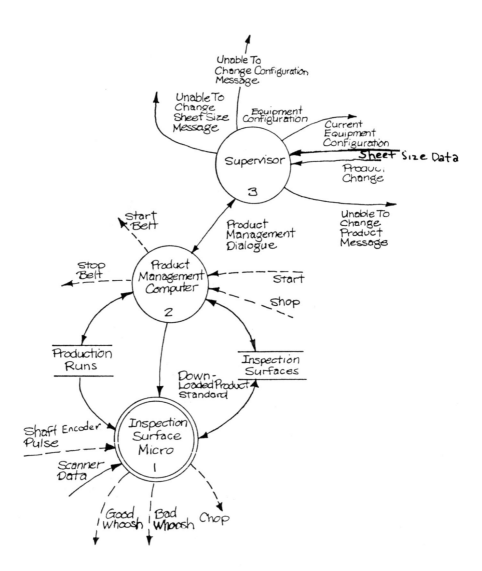

Figure D.0 Defect inspection system processors.

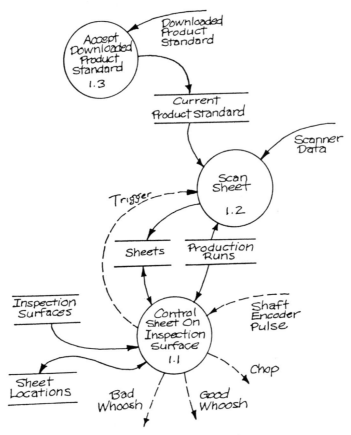

Figure D.1 Inspection surface micro.

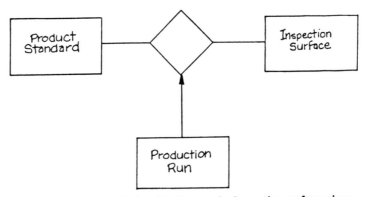

Figure D.1.ER Entity-relationship diagram for inspection surface micro.

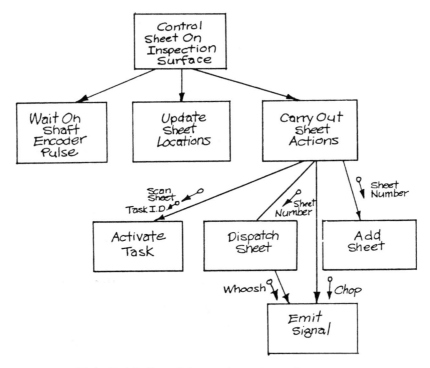

Figure D.1.1 Control sheet on inspection surface.

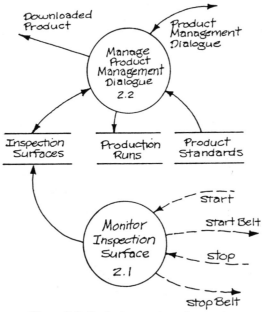

Figure D.2 Product management computer.

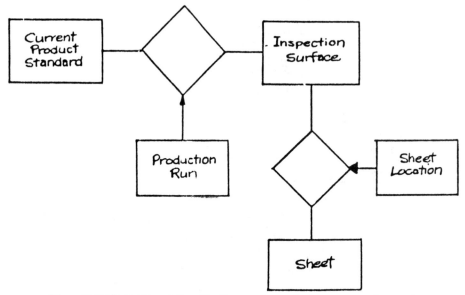

Figure D.2.ER Entity-relationship diagram for product management computer.

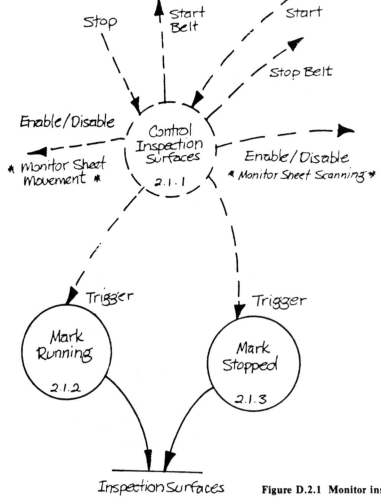

Figure D.2.1 Monitor inspection surface.

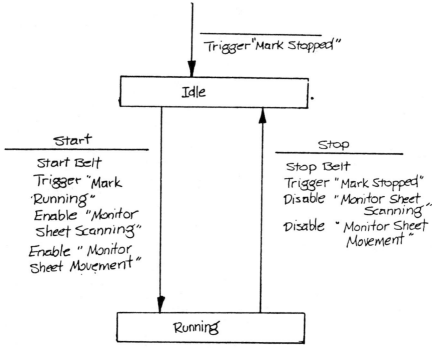

Figure D.2.1 Control inspection surfaces.

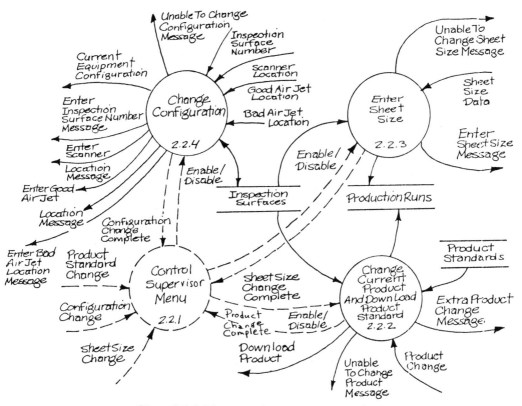

Figure D.2.2 Manage product management dialogue.

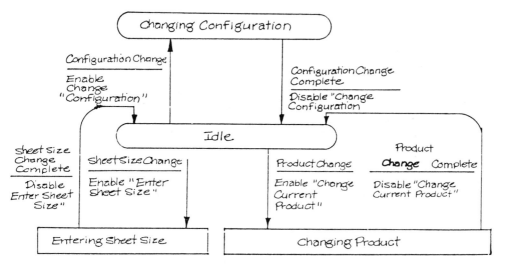

Figure D.2.2.1 Control supervision menu.

Data Dictionary

configuration change = **

configuration change complete = **

configuration data entry messages = enter good airjet location message +
enter bad airjet location message +
enter scanner location message +
enter inspection surface number message

configuration dialogue = configuration change + equipment configuration:
current equipment configuration +
unable to change configuration message +
configuration data entry messages

current product standard = product standard

current product standard = product standard

enter bad airjet location message = **

enter good airjet location message = **

enter good airjet location message = **

enter inspection surface number message = **

enter product change messsage = **

enter scanner location message = **

enter sheet size message = **

inspection surface number = **

product change complete = **

product change dialogue = product standard change + product change
enter product change message +
unable to change product message

product management dialogue = sheet size dialogue + configuration dialogue +
product change dialogue

sheet size change = **

sheet size change complete = **

sheet size dialogue = sheet size change + sheet size data:
enter sheet size message +
unable to change sheet size message

unable to change sheet size message = **

INDEX